OVERVIEW OF THE BO

MW01100495

Over 100 my true short stories from my life.

Stories of my encounters with GOD.
Stories of my conversations with GOD.
Stories of my arguments with GOD.
Stories of my meetings with GOD in Israel.

Stories of miracles.
Stories of depression.
Stories of discipline.
Stories of love.
Stories of life.

Along the way I have pondered these questions:

• Is there really a GOD and if so, does HE care about me?
• **Is Jesus really the only way? GOD Himself answers this one!**
• What is the purpose of my life?

Yes, I did tell GOD HE was wrong.
I have told GOD it was HIS problem and HIS fault.
I screamed at GOD and have told HIM to leave me alone.
We all have, not so much in our words like me, but in our
actions.

I trust you will find this book as valuable in your journey as
I have in remembering and reliving the awesome stories.

The cover picture is of my eldest Son and two eldest
Grandsons hiking up to Eva Lake in
Revelstoke National Park, British Columbia, Canada.

You are welcome to contact me if you wish at any of these:

Email: therockkelowna@gmail.com
Lives in: Kelowna, Canada

INDEX of STORIES: (I highlighted my favourites)   Page

STORY # 1 in 1999: GOD said to me:

GOD said to me:"*I want to show you something amazing!!!*
Tell your son Chris to raise his arms up. "

My son Chris and I were standing on the top of a snow capped totally clouded in mountain at the edge of the Canadian Rockies in early summer of 1999. I was almost 50 years old and my son in his mid 20's when I heard GOD say that to me. I took my camera out and started to take pictures as I explained to Chris what GOD had said. **Chris said he heard HIM too**, so he did, he raised his long arms straight up.

At first, I could see just a glimpse of sunlight directly below us looking straight down likely some 3,000 feet to prairies below and the clouds started to open up. Then the clouds opened up about ten feet wide from our feet and cut a path making a narrow blue sky pathway to the eastern horizon framed with billowing white clouds. **Then the clouds rolled back like a scroll until we could see all around**. We could see the prairies to the east and the jagged Rocky Mountains and glaciers behind us with the bright blue sky against the mountains white snow.

In amazement and awe Chris, not realizing it, had lowered his arms to his side. The clouds rolled back in again and we stood there in silence and awe. It all lasted about as long as it took you to read this. I heard a roll of thunder and said: "A storm is coming in, we need to get down off this mountain top" and we headed down.

We were GLOWING from our mountain top experience.

Years later Chris's Mom, Gwen, framed a picture of Chris she really liked as she said he just glowed. She asked me where that picture was taken. I checked the old negatives and it was on top of that mountain and it was the last one on that roll.

I have those pictures framed and on my wall to remind me, daily.

STORY # 2:   FEAR WINS:

We came down about a thousand feet off the mountain peak and came across a hole in the rocks. Chris stopped there and said this was the reason He had brought me up there to see. Going to the mountain top was just a spontaneous thing, **a GOD moment**.

Those moments are so easily missed if we are too focused on our purpose.

We crawled through the small opening in the rock and climbed nearly straight down hanging onto a rope for likely 50 feet. At the bottom was an amazing network of caves carved out by glacier flow. The rock around the cave looked like the inside of a metal culvert with those rings of waves.   We got out our flashlights and started to hike down into the depths of the mountain. We came across many forks and we decided that we should always go to the left at each fork and then when we return we will only go right and find our way back. It sounded like a good plan at the time. We also tried to make markers with rocks but it was very dark and it seemed the darkness just swallowed up our flashlight's light.

We turned around after some time and headed back always going right now at any fork. Then the unthinkable happened when we found a triple fork. My mind started to race in fear. I did not remember any triple forks. **Which fork had we come out of?**

A wrong decision and we could be wandering the miles of caves forever or at least until the flashlight batteries died. We would then be totally lost in the utter darkness within the depths of the earth. We would not be able to know if we were above or below the exit and going towards or away. Also, no one knew where we were or was expecting us home for days.

I had a panic attack of fear like I have never experienced. How embarrassing. I was stricken and terrified with fear. Only an hour before GOD had miraculously parted the clouds for us and now I had totally lost faith and did not even give GOD a thought. Shame on me.

It reminded of when Elijah after his miraculous Mount Carmel experience ran and hid in a cave in fear when Queen Jezebel threatened to kill him.

I will not criticize or judge Elijah anymore, I was no better.

Just then we heard some voices. Chris shouted out into the darkness. "Hello? Anyone there?" A voice replied "Chris, is that you?" It was John, Chris's roommate back at Briercrest Bible College in Saskatchewan which was years ago and a thousand miles away. To get to this cave we had taken an old forestry road to a parking place and then hiked up a nearly abandoned trail. It was hours out of the little village of Nordegg where Chris was doing Pastoral summer relief at a church. Nordegg is on a side road between Banff and Jasper in the middle of nowhere in the Canadian Rockies.

John was at the entrance of the cave. The reason I never saw the third fork was we had come in there at a 90 degree angle from the entrance which intersected the main cave. Had we not seen that third fork in that darkness, we would have just kept walking. Just around the corner of that fork toward the voice we left the invading darkness and went up into the daylight shining down the small hole we had crawled down.

Now we were storming back up to the world of light. Saved.

To think that just an hour or so before GOD had talked to me and showed me something unbelievably awesome by parting the clouds. A brief time later in the cave my faith escaped me as fear overwhelmed me in the depths of the rock just to have someone show up right at that moment to lead us out. **Out of the darkness and into the light.**

God's hand was all over everything that day, _as always,_ whether I knew it or not.

Story #3: GOD has prepared GOOD THINGS for ME to do: Courtenay from 1994-1996, I am mid-40's

The job I swore I would never do again turned out to be likely the biggest growth and blessing for me ever. Never say never.

I have hesitated in writing this section as it is just too much to try and tackle. Tears are swelling up as I start in amazement that GOD would care this much to include me is his Awesome plan. Whether you believe these stories or not is immaterial to me. They are true with many witnesses and if anything, understated.

The Cumberland Boys Club was founded by Stan Porritt with the Canadian Sunday School Mission (CSSM) back in about 1977 and was every Thursday night when school was in. Basically it was floor hockey for the under privileged boys of Cumberland. Cumberland at the time was considered a "welfare town" by the "good folk" of Courtenay and Comox.

I finally got out of working on the road where I had lost all confidence in who I was and what I could do. **I have learned that a person whose confidence is broken, is totally broken.**

I was getting back into a bank branch so I could do what I loved best, working with staff and clients to be the best we could be. This was not just any branch, this was the Courtenay Branch. I was fired there back in 1984 (story later) but the staff still loved me and most of our friends still lived there.

How wonderful that with all our traveling, in the very low and depressing time I was in, we were getting to "GO HOME". To me, the Comox Valley was home. When I pulled into town I stopped at the old steam engine that was at the entrance to Courtenay and thanked GOD for such a blessing, and promised:

I would do what HIS will was.

Story #4. My craziest NEGOTIATING with GOD story ever.

I was staying at our friend's house until my wife Gwen could moved to Courtenay and we moved into our house which was being constructed. Best house we had ever had.

Don Beeler called and said he was sure glad I was back as he really needed help with the Cumberland Boys Club. I had initially helped Stan Porritt of the Canadian Sunday School Mission with the boys club back in 1978 to 1984. Stan left around 1981 and I took it over and then Don came and helped me until I left the area to move to Greenwood with the bank in 1984. For 10 years Don had run it.

I told Don, *NO WAY !!!* I had not come back to go backwards and run a boys club. I wanted to move up the ladder (so to speak) and be active in men's ministry instead. I put a quick stop to that as I knew he would be calling.

A few days later, I think it was a Friday night, I got a call from Leslie, Don's wife. She said Don had just had a heart attack and they had no one to run the boys club on Thursday and not enough time to cancel, could I run it until he was back on his feet?

What about his team I asked, as you can't run a 30-40 boys club with ages from 8-18 without 6-8 good men. We went down the list of their team, one's father had died (or something) and he had to go back east to help his mother, another just lost his job and was out of town looking for work, another ...... until she had gone thru the whole crew and not one man was left to help.

What do you say to good friend's wife in her time of distress? Don had had a heart attack and was in the hospital and his wife Leslie had a burden with the boys club. It appeared only I could help, as I knew how to run it .... So I said "Sure, I'll look after it, don't worry."

So I needed a crew. I remembered how hard it was to get help as many of the men we took out to the club would only last one night. They could not handle what seemed to be very rough kids from the other side of the tracks, as they thought. I just saw them as kids.

I remembered the kids from when I ran it back 10 years before. I had the old red 1969 Dodge Econo Van and could put 17 kids standing in the back. I dropped them all off at home or if the streets were covered in snow, drag them on a long rope snow skiing home. Such fun, can't do that kind of thing now, probably shouldn't have then.

Many times Billy would say: "I don't live here anymore, I live with Jimmy now, and he's my new brother". I remembered one nice churchly gentleman from Courtenay who came up to Stan and said a kid pulled knife on him when he called a penalty. Stan, a no nonsense camp cook asked: "Well… did you take the knife away from him?" I can still hear Stan say that and almost break into laughter myself. The nice Courtenay Church Gentleman turned around and walked out to the gym, never to be seen again. We had gone thru a lot of well-meaning Christian men but it was hard to get helpers as the group had a "tuff" reputation. Now if you knew me, I never got into a fight at school and avoided confrontation. This was not my world either.

So as I sat on the floor thinking how I was going to get help, I was flipping thru the local paper when an advertisement caught my eye. A new church had started up. They were meeting in the college auditorium and everyone was welcome. I circled it and thought, there… new blood, maybe these guys had never heard of the Cumberland Boys Club and I could get some help. I didn't think I had any chance with the other churches as we had drained all them. So I went to the new Alliance Church.

It was in the theatre style seats at the new college. I wandered in, said hi to a few and sat down on the first row and listened. I had a note pad with me and took it out. "Ok GOD, here I am. You know I didn't want to do the boys club but I am basically being forced into it so I need a little help here. I need at least 5 helpers. Here is my paper, you tell me who." Then we have to figure out how you ask. Do I Say "Oh, I know you don't know me, but I need some help with a boys club that I haven't been to for 10 years." "Oh, and by the way GOD, one of them has to have his St. John's Ambulance ticket as mine had expired and I do not have time to renew by Thursday night."

The main door into the auditorium was right beside me and the pastor stood there greeting people as they came in and called them by name. In walked the first gentlemen ... Good morning pastor Dave, good morning Frank.

I wrote down Dave and Frank. GOD said, *"No and no. First, Dave is the pastor and he is just starting this church, he will support you and help in event of emergency but he is not to be one of your helpers"*.

"Ok, how about Frank I asked?" I asked. God said, *"NO not Frank."* I questioned GOD on that and I said "Yes Frank, I love him already, he is my kind of guy, he came in loud and friendly to all. Are you sure GOD?" I was not exactly telling GOD He was wrong, but just questioning HIS judgement. Frank became a good personal friend but not a key person at the club. So I scratched the two names off.

God said:*" I will tell you who."* Then in came other men and I got confirmation of more guys which were OK'd by GOD. Well, that is four plus me makes five, I need one more or I stand at the door Thursday night and tell the kids it's closed.

All had come in and no other names were given to me. I told GOD, "We need one more or no deal." They closed the doors and started the church service. Halfway thru the first song in walked a couple. This was a small church with few people as they were just starting and it was fairly informal.

The pastor stopped us singing and sarcastically but with all the love in the world (you would have to know Dave, he's the only guy I know that could pull this off and actually use it to endear himself) "Well... Paul.... I am so glad you could make it.. Have a seat my friend and we will start again." GOD flooded my soul with *"Paul is your KEY man, big time"*. I was blown away and wrote down Paul.

I have the names now how do I talk to them. They mentioned they were going to be having a men's breakfast on Tuesday morning at some restaurant. OK, that seemed like a good opportunity to discuss. So I told GOD that I would go to the breakfast and if we were to run the Cumberland Club all the men on my list would need to be there and I would agree. Wait, one more thing. Paul, if he is my key man, would have to sit right across from me.

So on Tuesday I was very excited and very nervous. What would I say? I got to the restaurant early so I could pick my seats. I moved a table for 6 a little off to the side so we could talk in private. I told GOD; "Ok, you bring these guys on my list to this table." I would say nothing to them till they were all seated at that table. I thought I would make it that much harder so I sat at the end of table for 6 and reminded GOD that Paul had to sit across from me. Too hard you say? Hey, GOD is GOD. Don't underestimate HIM? In they came, the Pastor, Frank and the other guys on my list and many other guys but no Paul.

The appropriate men sat at my table, but still no Paul. When Frank came over he greeted me big time like he always had and sat in "the seat" right across from me. We ordered and eat. Well GOD, no Paul and I have Frank in "the seat". Of all the people and I still disagreed with GOD and thought Frank would be the best man for my key man. We finished eating and got our coffees to get into chatting… So how do you take over someone else's men's breakfast and ask them to help you with the Boys club? Especially with Frank in the key seat. But then I wouldn't need to as Frank was sitting where Paul had to be so I guess **I just cancel the boys club**.

All of a sudden Frank jumped up and shouted, "Oh man… I gotta go, I was supposed to pick up my wife Gerta and take her to the doctors this morning." He jumped up and ran for the door. When he opened the door in his hurry he bumped into a man coming in and almost knocked him off his feet. He apologized by saying: "I'm so sorry Paul, but I gotta go…. But I've warmed a seat for you by that new guy, Deryl" The only seat that was empty was that one across from me, and Paul, a man I had never met was to become the best man I have every worked with. GOD's man for the job.

I told them my story and they all agreed. I did not find out much about Paul's qualification for many months later, as he was almost shutdown quiet. I never asked as I did not need to know, as he was GOD's pick and if Paul screwed up, it was GOD's fault, not mine. I still didn't want to do the job. I don't think Don Beeler ever came back.

Paul had worked far up north, counselling underprivileged kids, just like we were to do, was some type of pastor and was an ambulance driver with all the first aid licenses we would ever need. Paul had gone thru a crisis and like me, only worse, he was just coming out the other side. This was the perfect job to help him and me.

Paul and I worked as one. We could run that gym floor and not even need to share words. We knew what the other needed before asked and did it. I have never had anyone work so well with before or since. **He was a GOD send.** I would say off the cuff that we worked and built up the club for 10 yrs but when I thought about it, it was only two years. But by the grace of GOD we did 10 years work in those 2 years. I just took a few minutes off to re-do the math as I cannot believe it was only two years.

An amazing story of how to build an awesome team. I only wish all my life was that simple on how to follow GOD's will. This story is only a start of so many unbelievable things God did in those two years.

GOD provided.

#5: GOD WOKE ME UP from a lazy summer's day SNOOZE.

One Sunday afternoon I was lying on the couch watching golf on TV with my eyes closed when I heard GOD say that HE needed me to do something. "What?" I asked, *"Just go and I'll show you"* GOD said.

So I got in my car and started driving. Ok, I think I know what GOD wants. I was working with a man and he was likely having a bad day, therefore he would be at the Arbutus Pub, right next to my bank. No, He wasn't there. I had parked at the bank so thought, maybe he is in the Instant Bank machine getting more money for his booze. No, not in the bank area. So I got in my car and started to drive. GOD said *"turn this way"* then that, in and out of alleyways and roads I didn't know existed. I felt like I was in a fog and finally I pulled out and drove down a road when GOD said *"stop here."* I pulled over and parked.

I looked around to see where we were. I recognized that we were right in front of my friend's Paul's apartment. He lived on the second floor of an older apartment building. He lived in Courtenay on Cumberland Rd which is on the road to Cumberland. **I realized that anytime my car was pointed towards Cumberland, (GOD's will for me to do) things went well.**

I got out of my car and looked at Paul's window. I noticed his lights were out so said to GOD , "He's not home." GOD said, *"Open your trunk"*. I said: Why ? He said *"take out your football."* I told GOD He was wrong as I don't have a football anymore, I had lost it in the move. I looked around in the trunk and it was hidden up against the side.

GOD said: *"Throw the football at the front door entrance of the apartment."*. Yeah sure, right. Oh well, no one was around, so if I threw it, then I could go retrieve it and go back home and lay on the couch. The front door of the apartment was about the full distance away that I could throw a football. So I pulled back and threw a perfect pass right for the door.

The doorway and walkway was likely down about 3 feet under ground level and now I realized it was all a big plate glass window. Oh well, this wouldn't be the first window I had broken with a ball but how would I explain that to the police and insurance? GOD told me to do it? Yeah right, call the paddy wagon boys.

As the ball was in mid air the front door opened and Paul stepped out. I yelled: "catch it" and he did. He cradled the ball and tears rolled down his checks. Oh that feels good he says, he told me he used to love to play football in school.

I explained to him the weird story as to why I was there and told him my car was pointing to Cumberland. I asked if he wanted to come with me and see what the Lord had in store for us. I suggested that if we meet up with three teens (kind of the gang leaders) that we were working with under the Cumberland Boys club floor hockey in the winter we would know we were on the right track.

We went up and wandered the streets of Cumberland and ended up throwing the football around at the park in town. As soon as we started, those same three teens came over the hill, saw us and yelled, "Hey Godman, can we join you?" He thought he was insulting me when he called me Godman, but I was honoured.

We started our summer recreational program in the park and had an awesome summer.

We need to listen and obey.

Story # 6: ALL HELL BROKE LOOSE

Sometimes it seems like ALL HELL breaks loose and we don't understand it. Look up and learn.

Things were going well at the Cumberland Boys Club. I had a perfect team of guys working with me and the attendance had grown so that we had to expand to three clubs. I think we hit 120 one night. Ages 6-9, 10-13, and then 14-18 and we did all on Thursday night. Started at 5:00 and went to 10:00 I think, a big commitment but we were pleasantly exhausted when done.

Then the troubles started. A group opposed to us using the Community Hall/Gym as we were Christian based and during our devotional time were preaching religion on community property. They took it up with City Council and proposed they take it over.

The boys were getting rougher, fighting became the norm, continual swearing at each other. Girls would sit in the bleacher when the older boys were there and very distracting and interrupting. The occasional drug dealer would show up and boys would sneak out the back door to get a high.

It all came to head one night as everything seemed to go wrong. Swearing, fighting, bleeding noses, drug dealers and kids coming and going. We had lost total control and chaos ruled. **It was as if all of Hell had broken loose and we had lost.**

Near the end of the evening I had had it. I stormed into the boys washroom/change room (no one was in there) and I blew up at GOD! I slammed the bathroom doors and then pounded on the walls **screaming** at HIM. **" I CAN'T DO THIS, IT IS TOO MUCH, I HAVE LOST TOTAL CONTOL, I AM NOT EQUIPPED FOR THIS, I NEVER WANTED TO DO THIS IN THE FIRST PLACE, IT WAS YOUR IDEA….. YOU FIXED IT !!!!!!!!**

And I stormed out.

I closed the club early that night and went home, ready to quit.

With dread the next Thursday I showed up. I couldn't believe it. The people trying to close us down did not show up to protest or ever did again. The girls didn't show up to interrupt and distract the boys or ever did again. We never saw the drug dealer again. No one SWORE, no one fought, they played amazing floor hockey and had fun. During devotions everyone sat down and listened. I was stunned, I talked to the crew and they were stunned too. Someone said it was like we had guardian angels on each of the corners of the building protecting us.

We had connected with the local Youth for Christ as they had a very large presence in the Comox Valley and I had become good friends with the leader Brian Hemp. He is an awesome man of GOD. I attended the quarterly meeting and when it came time to give my brief, I told them the above story. When I finished, a lady, one of our prayer partners who had been sitting doing her knitting, spoke up.

"Yes Deryl, we heard you were having some trouble, so a number of ladies went out to Cumberland Commuity Hall during the week and laid hands on it. We each went to the four corners of the building and asked for GOD's anointing and protection."

WOW…. I was speechless. Thank you Lord.

From that point, the club moved quickly forward. We had a whole crew of supporters attend a City Council meeting and I explained the difference between what the other group that was proposing to take over and what we offered. I said that the Cumberland Boys Club had been running regularly since 1977 until now, (being 1996) over 20 years. One of the longest running successful programs in Cumberland. Yes, we are Christian based and we try and teach the boys Christian moral, such as sportsmanship, loving and caring for others etc… I said to City Council that you can go with the others but as you all know, dealing with 100 or so of the Cumberland kids is not an easy task. Cumberland takes pride in its reputation as Dodge City and the kids like to live up to that reputation.

We are Christians and believe we have a higher calling. **A calling from GOD himself to help these boys.** This is why we have been faithful for over 20 years serving this community and not asking for anything but the use of the gym.

Council voted to allow us to use the gym and even gave us permission to say anything we wanted during our devotional. A big break from before.

Next we were given the keys to an almost abandoned church. The congregation was getting older and invited us in. We managed to bring in the boys and years later some of the boys were more excited about attending a bible study and prayer than to play floorhockey. Beyond my comprehension.

The change took place when I had my blow out in the bathroom with GOD. I started nearly ever phrase with "I". I can't take it... I, I , I and finally I gave it all up and threw it in GOD's face for HIM to "FIX IT !". I think GOD finally smiled and said: "you finally get it". This is MY work, GOD's work, trust in ME and I will FIX IT.

And HE did.

Story # 7: GOD or PORN, who will I serve ?
Gibsons in 1996-1998

GOD IS A JEALOUS GOD, and Disciplines His Children.

How easy it is to be thrown off my game,
to lose my focus, my purpose by a simple distraction.

I had just finished an amazing 2 years serving GOD doing the Cumberland Boys Club. Anytime I was having trouble at work, at home or just a bad day, I would point my car to Cumberland and it would all turn out right.

Then one day after about 2 years doing the Cumberland Boys Club GOD came along and said: ***"It is time for you go."*** I protested: "No, you cannot pull me from the game now." It is like pulling a baseball pitcher having a shutout in the bottom of the ninth of the World Series. But GOD said I was not the man to do the rest of the work and that HE had another man in mind. Yes, I know I said, Stefan... but Lord, I have tried to bring Stefan on board and he won't even talk to me. ***" I know,"*** said GOD, ***"that is why you have to leave so that he will come.....* "** "OK" I replied.

I went to work and the boss called me into his office. Two years before He had hired me to take his branch from the old style banking into the new sales age of banking. We did a marvelous job, but now he said, we received next year's budget and we do not have room for the two managers. Knowing GOD had already pulled me from Cumberland Boys Club I might as well throw in the towel at the Bank too. So I said: "Well, let me go, you have two young kids and I am confident I will find another job, it is time for me to move on."

I got a new job at the Bank just across the water at Gibsons, BC, home of the Beachcombers TV series. Beautiful place on the Sunshine Coast and just a short ferry ride into Vancouver.

When I pulled into town GOD said "*I have new job for you. I want you to build an Alcohol Free Youth Lounge. A safe place where teenagers and young adults can hang out. Pull over.*"

I pulled over into a parking lot and was on the key intersection of town and there was a nice warehouse type or more like an abandoned strip mall. *"This is the place"* HE said.

I drove away thinking how on earth would this happen. I knew no one and I didn't have an extra $100.00 to spare with just changing jobs and didn't know anything about running a place like that. Oh well I figured, that is GOD's problem if HE wants to get it done.

A few days passed and a man came to my office. He was a realtor and said GOD had asked him to talk to me and that he wanted to give me use of one of his buildings. He asked if I would be able to meet with him Thursday night and go see it. "Would love to" I said.

When I got home to the new the house we had bought I noticed the neighbor washing his car. I went over and introduced myself. We got chatting and I found out he attended the church we thought of attending and that he was the worship leader. He said the worship band and even some of the other churches worship bands met at a place on Thursday nights and practice and jam together. I should come. I said I would love to but was busy that Thursday.

Thursday night the Realtor picked me up and took me to his building. "The building" of course that GOD had already said HE would give me. We went to go inside and we heard music. My neighbor and his crew were inside playing music. I gathered everyone around and told them my story and what GOD wanted to do. They were all excited, especially when the Realtor said he would pay for all the renovations. We all dreamed as we walked around planning it out.

That night at home I was up in the upper room where I set up my computer. It was late at night and my wife was having a long bath or had already gone to bed. I wondered, was it true what I had heard about this new thing, the internet and the world wide web.

This was the first time I had internet connection. Was it true that you could get porn, free, no hassle, no going to the drug store magazine or strip clubs with the chance of being seen? I typed in the search and waiting as the old dialup slowly revealed. The image that appeared fried my brain and is still there today over 20 years later. I was hooked. Maybe that is where the word hookers comes from? The next morning I was driving to work. I can remember like it is happening right now. I am driving up the hill and GOD shows up. He says, *"I didn't like what you did last night "*. "That's your problem" I said defensively. God said, *"I cannot have you doing MY work and working with MY young people if you are going to fill your mind and thoughts with porn"*. I replied, "I am up in my own small very private room late at night, not bothering anyone." God said, *"You have to choose, if want to continue with the porn, then I will have to withdraw MY support from you and what I have given you."*

I foolishly replied "Do what you have to, but I am NOT stopping."

I am sure any of you reading this would say, **what an IDIOT !!!.** But I am sure we have all done a similar thing. You may not have a conversation like I do with GOD but if you do things you know that HE is against, is that any different?

Your actions speak as loud as my words.

God is a jealous God. The first commandment is "do not have any other gods before me" and Jesus said: "Love the Lord your God with all your heart, soul and mind ..." So if my thoughts are totally consumed by something else, in my opinion, that becomes my god and GOD will become jealous of that. We hear alot about GOD is love in church today. GOD loves you... and that is good. HE does, but GOD is much more than what our society today calls "love".
GOD is just,
GOD is pure,
GOD is HOLY !
GOD does get angry and
GOD gets jealous, jealous for you, for me.

Back to the story: I arrived at work to find my realtor friend waiting for me. He said, "I am so sorry Deryl but after our meeting last night someone made me an offer on that property that I just could not refuse. So I sold it. Sorry, but you will have to find another place."

I thought, wow, I better tell my neighbour. I mentioned to him to tell his crew as they were making plans too. He said it didn't matter anyway, as after I left they got in a dispute over what it would all look like. The worship team at that church split.

I was attending a 5:00 am Thursday men's prayer. That early as most of the guys caught the 1st ferry as they worked in Vancouver. One morning the two leaders got into a disagreement. They were both older retired men. One of a Pentecostal background and the other of an Anglican background. The one said your prayers are always the same, no passion, likely out of a book... the other replied your prayers are just show, full of pretend passion, flowery words and mostly non-sense. The argument grew louder till they pushed the table away that separated them and literally started to wrestle. I could not believe my eyes. That ended that prayer session and any future.

Numerous other things happened and much of it related to porn with others as well but so as not to breach confidentiality I will leave those stories unsaid. But that church had a split.

Things at work started to go the wrong, big time. I was going to get a sub-standard report which for a guy used to getting top awards in the District, Province and even Country, this was not going down well. It also was a time when the under-performers were being culled. Fired if I am being too politically correct. After 28 years of breathing and living the company and working 50-60 or even 80 hours a week if needed with no extra pay, this was coming down hard on me.

So many things were going on I won't go into all the details but basically **all the things that I prided myself in were being pulled out from under me as worthless.** One at a time. I was scrambling in panic. Finally in an act of desperation and before my whole world caved in ....likely just to prove I was still in control...

I quit.

My wife had had enough. Enough of my anger, enough of my yelling and frustration at the world and she said she was going to stay with a friend for awhile. She left.

I spent the next four days on the couch under a blanket just crying.

OK GOD... I am sorry, please forgive me.

GOD does forgive but there are still consequences for our actions. I was unemployed, nearly broke and was not expecting a good referral from my 28 year employer. My wife did come back after about four days and we started to rebuild. Rebuild our marriage, rebuild our finances and

rebuild our relationship with GOD.

8: My brother LLOYD, can you FORGIVE YOURSELF

Not all stories have a good ending. 1994

There is an old Eskimo story of a Grandfather teaching his Grandson as they were out hunting. He was teaching him how to hunt so they could live, but also teaching him how to live. They were watching a pair of wolves from a distance fighting over their kill.

The GrandFather said: "Within each of us there are like two wolves fighting for survival. A good wolf and a bad wolf."
The Grandson asked: "Which one wins ? "
The Grandfather said: **"The one you feed the most."**

Lloyd is my older brother. He is about 20 years older than I am and in a lot of ways the man I have looked to in life for my guidance. My decision on who I married, my career, my wife's career or that she was a stay at home Mom, my faith, my golf, my drinking and most important, my character were based on influence from my brother Lloyd.

To feed the good wolf and to watch out for the bad wolf within me.

He was more like my father than my father. My Father was 43 years older than me and more like my Grandfather. I did not know any of my actual Grandfathers as they had passed away before I had any memory of them.

Also, personality and attributes, I think I am more like Lloyd than anyone else I know.

Lloyd married Helen back in 1950 or so and had 3 sons, Blake, Ross & Blair. Blake, my nephew was only a few months younger than me and growing up we were more like brothers than uncle and nephew.

They lived with us for a time when I was in Grade 2 and then in our early teen years we attended their church where Lloyd was the pastor, Ellendale Baptist in Surrey, now called Cedar Grove. I would normally spend the weekend at their place and we would go golfing or whatever, most time with Lloyd.

In the 1960's when Lloyd was ages 30-40 **he created an excellent reputation for himself.** His church was growing, he was in great demand as a guest speaker throughout the area, a professor in the Bible College and he even had his own radio talk show where he loved to get into a dispute with whoever would dare to call. He had a very sharp and highly educated and knowledgeable mind.

His fame and glory took its toll on his ministry. His pride became the driving force in my opinion. In a letter he wrote at age 62 he acknowledges after the fact that "Thirty years ago, and prior to that, I read and kept myself informed for the sake of being able to competently with rational discernment dispense the truths of GOD. I was able to give an answer for all we hold. I did this, for, what I see now, **personal pride in my knowledge. Knowing for knowing.**" (Being smarter than anyone else, superior)

In 1968 at the peak of his glory and at the age of about 38 he lost all this. His ministry at the church, the college professor job, the radio station talk show, his wife and to some extent, his boys.

But that Priebe did not lose his pride.

Unemployed and unemployable in the Christian community because of his actions and attitude, my Dad gave him a job on his construction site building the school in Langley. He was partnered with me and he was the carpenter and I was his apprentice. I spent the next year or so, one on one with my brother Lloyd listening to his story.

I was going to say most of it I will not repeat, but then again, I have heard the same story so many times from so many other guys since then. It seems, those disenfranchised or who have left the church find me, especially pastors. I think we have all had our frustrations with the church and more specifically the attitude and actions of those we believe should be better. The question is, how have you responded? Run away, angry and vocal or have you chosen to just forgive and love people where they are, **in their own spiritual journey.**

Lloyd did not lose his pride but rather poured his anger at the church and at GOD on the injustice and ignorance of their actions in rejecting him.

After the job in Langley was done I got married and joined the Bank. One cold miserable rainy day, while laying forms in the mud and ice, I told my boss, I said "Dad, this is not the life for me and that I was going to find an inside job."

Lloyd moved on as well and he became a Real Estate salesman. He was a charmer and he could sell ice to Eskimos. He joined up with what was then Block Brothers, one of the largest firms back then and a shirt tail relative of ours. Lloyd quickly became top salesman and they put him in charge of training the new guys. He was back on his game and definitely did NOT need GOD to restrict his abilities and opportunities. He could do it on his own and the wealth poured in.

His 2nd marriage did not last.

Lloyd achieved all any great salesman could ever want. Money, fame and adoration but the cost personally was showing up in his loneliness with the loss of his family, purpose and relationship with GOD. He took to drinking, or I should say, drinking more. His drinking and attitude lost him his real-estate job and income which only increased the addiction to alcohol.

He lost most of his pocessions as the alcohol became his master and he ended up pretty much living in his old beat up car on skid row. My brothers would seek him out, sober him up and give him a job in construction with them only to have him slip back into his old ways.

One night, May 30, 1994, I was visiting my Mom at her apartment near Gilford Mall in Surrey and the phone rang. It was one of my other brothers calling as he knew I was there. He asked me to tell Mom that they had found Lloyd in his chair, alone, dead.

My Mom who was 85 years old collapsed in my arms and we wept. She said a parent should never outlive their children. She asked me if Lloyd would be in heaven or was his sin so bad that GOD would reject him. I said, "Mom, after all Lloyd had done, do you still love him and is he still your son?" She said of course, no matter what, she would always love him and he would always be her son. I said, "Then how much more would our heavenly Father who loves us, still love Lloyd then too and welcome him home."

9: My brother Lloyd's LAST SERMON.

Lloyd wrote a letter some months before he died. **His last sermon I like to think.** I know he really struggled with the verse that says for those that were enlightened and fall away. He believe he was in that position and for a long time he lived in that anguish, finding it hard to forgive himself, that there is no second chance. But in Lloyd's letter he wrote:

"In the past twenty days I have with intense hunger – read, studied and pursued books and the BOOK (The Bible) with a pure motive, not to learn ABOUT GOD but TO KNOW GOD. Believe on the name of Jesus Christ and you will be saved. This will forever cement, make perfect and securely establish your position before and with GOD.

My position in that day before Almighty GOD is secured and satisfied by the sacrifice of Christ on the cross and my faith therein." *This satisfied God in respect to my place in eternity. "*

Further in his letter, he writes what I think is a critical thing. Funny, I had never read his letter though it has been in my drawer for almost 25 years until today. I borrowed it from his son Ross and I always meant to return it but guess I was to keep it until today for this. He comes to the very same conclusion at age 62 as me, I am 65. Our struggles with sex, booze, our jobs, people, the church, GOD and especially pride are so closely linked, even the time frames of our lives match. The difference is, I have learned from his life and applied that lesson to try and improve mine so I don't fall into the same pit as my brother did.

His first conclusion is that his position before Almighty God is secured and satisfied by the sacrifice of Christ on the cross and my faith therein. Then he goes on to his 2nd conclusion:

"now comes the crunch, the acid test of my condition of life.

This is Part #2 of I John 3:23, ***"And that ye love one another"***
No exception !
No, "if only they !

No, if only you know him (her) as I do!
No, I would, BUT!
No, Maybe if!
No, that's easy for you to say, BUT, put yourself in my shoes.

Any reader who honestly has a problem with Part #2 of the new commandment-
"that we love on another, "
Is urged to slowly in contemplative meditation consider I Cor Ch. 13
(but the greatest of these is love)

For size of character, how does I Cor 13 fit ?
Is it too tight ?
Too Demanding ?
too narrow ?
these diving definitions of part #2 of the new commandment, - " that we love each other" are not relative definitions.

They are ABSOLUTE !

There are no secret inhibitions that would allow exceptions. There are no reservations that permit holdouts on certain defined attitudes and in I Cor 13.
No, I'll wait and see,
No I'll try,
No grey shades of relativity. I Cor 13, as it relates to your daily condition – your daily walk in life as it affects others is an absolute demand of God.

*Part #2 "that we love one another: **must reflect itself in every facet of life** – to everyone we meet. This is true from our relationship to our intimate mate to the most overt obnoxious persons we know. – How does 1 Cor 13 fit your walk, your condition, your attitude and actions to others?*

(see bottom of this section for all of I Cor 13)

I look back at my brother Lloyd's life and cry, what a waste. Such a great man of GOD with the greatest of potential to squander it all for a little sex and booze. The booze and rejection was the addiction he fed for 20 years until these 20 days when he sought GOD. But the greatest of his sins was his pride.

For the same thing that Lucifer fell from GOD's grace and likely in my mind **the greatest sin anyone can** commit is that they take pride in doing life themselves and that opens the doors for your weakness to distract you from your focus, your purpose, your spiritual opportunities that GOD created for you before the creation of the earth.

But thanks be to GOD who while we were sinners and had turned away from GOD, that GOD provided the sacrifice needed, that GOD knew we could not do, to redeem us so that we can be called the Sons of GOD.

Not all stories have a good ending... but
This one does, I believe,
Does have:

a happy ever after ending.

1 Corinthians 13: New International Version (NIV) in the Bible.

If I speak in the tongues of men or of angels, but do not have love, I am only a resounding gong or a clanging cymbal. If I have the gift of prophecy and can fathom all mysteries and all knowledge, and if I have a faith that can move mountains, but do not have love, I am nothing. If I give all I possess to the poor and give over my body to hardship that I may boast, but do not have love, I gain nothing.

Love is patient, love is kind. It does not envy, it does not boast, it is not proud. It does not dishonor others, it is not self-seeking, it is not easily angered, it keeps no record of wrongs. Love does not delight in evil but rejoices with the truth. It always protects, always trusts, always hopes, always perseveres.

Love never fails. But where there are prophecies, they will cease; where there are tongues, they will be stilled; where there is knowledge, it will pass away. For we know in part and we prophesy in part, but when completeness comes, what is in part disappears. When I was a child, I talked like a child, I thought like a child, I reasoned like a child. When I became a man, I put the ways of childhood behind me. For now we see only a reflection as in a mirror; then we shall see face to face. Now I know in part; then I shall know fully, even as I am fully known.

And now these three remain: faith, hope and love.
But the greatest of these is love.

Which wolf or spirit within you do you feed the most ?
Am I my brother's keeper? Yes.

I am sure my brother never realized what a major impact his actions, good and bad, would have on my life, as well as so many others. I had some asked about him just the other day, over 50 years since he left the ministry.

Live the life worthy of your calling.

Hebrews 12:1 *Therefore, since we are surrounded by such a great cloud of witnesses, let us throw off everything that hinders **and the sin that so easily entangles.** And let us run with perseverance the race marked out for us, fixing our eyes on Jesus, the pioneer and perfecter of faith.*

Story # 10: MY Brother VERN

I have had great respect for my older brother Vern all my life, except for one brief moment. I am the youngest of 8 boys and the age spread is 23 years from oldest to youngest, me. Vern is son # 3, great athlete, especially baseball and an inspiring preacher. My brother Lloyd, talked about above is son #2 was also a preacher and so is son #7, Glen and the rest were in construction, all except me.

Vern always struck me as a man who knew who he was. That he knew what he believed and was never afraid to stand up for it.

It was the day of our brother Lloyds funeral that this happened. Vern had taken the death far harder than I had. Understandable as he was closer to the same age and they grew up together and shared being Ministers together.   What bothered me was Vern was not, in my opinion, stepping up to the plate and supporting me in assuring Mom that Lloyd was now in heaven. He just said, "I don't know".

My wife Gwen had taken the car home already so I was getting a ride home with Vern in his old van. **A GOD thing I am sure.** I can still visualize and see that moment. I got in the passenger side and said something like, "Look Vern, you are the preacher and our Mom needs you to stand strong now, especially on the fact that Lloyd is now in heaven, to give her that assurance !!!"

Vern turned to me, nearly tears in his eyes and said, "I love you brother, I will not get into a heated argument with you." And he was silent.   I was furious, my strong brother, the one I had seen stand up to anyone was now being a coward, in my eyes.

Now I see it. He had found the truth, the truth was, that it was not his call. He is not called to judge, but to love. At this hour of great need, rather than stand his ground and fight for what he thought was right, he chose to just love me instead. He could see no good coming from a confrontation, of which no good would have come of it as I was totally wishing to have a major confrontation with him. To stand up for what I thought was right, even if I lost my brother.

You will know them by their love for each other, Jesus said.
Vern showed me Christ that day.

11: What will MY LEGACY be ?

I am writing this book of the stories of my life and my spiritual journey for my Children and Grandchildren. I know only a few stories of my Father and none of my Grand Fathers and I wish they had shared more of their spiritual journey.

That is why I am sharing mine.

It is said that the bad traits of a father become a legacy to his children to be repeated over and over to the 3rd and 4th generation until one of them takes the courage to break that chain.

I pray this is that moment.

It is also said that the blessing of a good father will be passed onto his children for a thousand generations.

Let the good blessings be my Legacy and Yours.

It is amazing to me how my children say and do things that I know I never said to them, never taught them or they never saw me do but they do exactly what I have done. Some call this "Soul-tie".

My journey will take us through many experiences and my numerous **direct and indirect encounters with GOD.** My encounters are both when I am on a religious mountain top high and when I am in the depths of the earth in my rebellious choices or in despair.

Is Jesus the only way or do all roads lead to GOD? The answer I got was direct from GOD Himself as I stood on Mountain Calvary.

One day my Mom and I were working on a Jigsaw puzzle. We had got the boarders done and then it seemed nothing was working. We went back and looked over all we had done and realized that one piece, though it looked right, was not. Because of that one wrong piece the whole picture could not be made and we were going to just give up.

I pray these stories will help you in your journey. If one part of the overall puzzle does not fit, then just take it out and put it to the side for now and work on the rest of the puzzle. One day you will find the right piece for that part as the overall pieces slowly come together.

12: Deryl's Spiritual Journey

I was born in Mission City, BC, Canada in the early 1950's to Harry and Clara Priebe. They were born in 1908 and 1909. My parents had their own spiritual journey. My Grandfather or Great Grandfather was the leader of a Mennonite community and Pastor of the church in Flowing Well, Saskatchewan. My Dad rebelled from the faith in his teens and early 20's as so many preacher kids do but re-embraced the faith in his mid-20's.

As I recall the story he rebelled big time. My Dad was a big strong farmer/construction man and 6'2" tall. He was married at 19 and had a few little kids but one night he was heading into town for a night of drinking and gambling. Apparently he had a serious problem with both. That night he came across a very tempting woman but before he could go deeper into trouble two men he had never seen before in their small Saskatchewan town escorted him out of the bar and out of town to go home to the family. He told me that at the edge of town when he turned around to confront the two men, they disappeared.

Dad said they were angels sent from GOD to turn him around. He vowed **to be the man GOD had made him to be** and he stopped drinking, stopped gambling and never looked at another woman. He turned his playing cards into scripture memorization cards and always carried a pack of these in his pocket to memorize.

I wish I knew more stories of my Dad as I know there were some awesome ones. He did not talk to me too much. That is why I am putting these GOD stories of mine into a book for my children, grandchildren and generations to come to read.

My parents worked a farm in Saskatchewan through the great depression and the dirty thirties. Near the end of World War II the farm burned down and they lost everything. They packed up the four boys and caught the train to BC as his brother-in-law got him a job helping to build the airport in Abbotsford. Around 1946 or so they moved out of what I call the Mennonite Colony known as Clearbrook across the river to Mission City. He built houses and then schools for most of his life in BC.

I have to admire and thank my Dad for taking that very courageous move to Mission City. Not only was he likely the first in over 400 years to leave the Mennonite Community but he also changed and started to attend a Baptist Church rather than a Mennonite Church.

It was the big break and a journey:

From German to English,
From Mennonite to Canadian,
From judging to forgiving,
From legalism to grace,
From rules to love.

Story # **13: BREAKING A 400 YEAR TRADITION:**

When my family moved to Mission we were leaving the very traditional and much regulated legalism to start a new spiritual life for the family that would be more Canadian and more full of grace as my Dad worked his way out from under the Old Testament type law. A mega move spiritually and I thank my Dad for having the foresight to do it. We even stopped speaking low German and only spoke English.

I look back at the rules and restrictions that my Dad grew up with to the liberated faith we have today and I am amazed.   It was considered wrong to smoke, drink alcohol, dance, go to movies, play cards or even billiards. It made no sense to me as King David of the Bible danced for the Lord and Jesus turned the water into wine at the wedding.

We are reading and following the same bible as my grandfathers but what changed and more important, what else should change?

One example I can remember was the family loved baseball. My Dad built us our own baseball diamond with backstop and everything and with 8 sons it was well used.

Sunday was to be the day of rest and respected. No sports were allowed on Sunday but Dad said he would amend to allow us to play "catch", "scrub" or "500 up" which is a kind of informal baseball, but we would not be allowed to have Teams. This, as I recall, was my first experience of breaking from the LAW and moving into the FREEDOM of Grace.

I love the movie "Fiddler on the Roof" as I can relate to it so well as the Father slowly allows the new things and bends old traditions of which he has no idea why they exist.

My Grandfathers lived in a Mennonite Community in Russia after moving there from Holland to Germany to Poland (old Prussia) and the Russia when Catherine the Great offered land to the Mennonites as they were greatly respected farmers. They left Russia to America around 1860 to avoid religious persecution.

Back to the movie where the Jewish Father living in Russia reaches a breaking point in his faith when his 3rd daughter wishes to marry a Russian. The first two daughters married within the faith, but not exactly according to old customs. The Father manages to talk his way around the various customs without losing his faith or being banished from the community.

But when the 3rd daughter wants to marry a Russian that is totally forbidden to marry outside of their Jewish faith. That scene or even thinking of that scene and I break into tears every time as it rips at my spiritual heart.

Where is that line?

Where is the truth, what is just ignorant tradition for the sake of control or misunderstanding?

What brings us closer to GOD and what breaks that true relationship with our Heavenly Father.

That is the fine line of these stories. In some stories I fail very dramatically but all have lead back to a deeper and more trusting relationship with GOD on my spiritual journey.

Like any child, we seem to always be pushing that line.

A quick funny story. I talked my Dad (and Mom) into going to the only movie I think he ever went to in his life. It was Fiddler on the Roof as I knew he would relate to it. Dad was so worried someone might see him as he was an Elder at the church. We got to the theatre and it was on Granville St. in downtown Vancouver. It was a crowded night so we had to stand outside for awhile in line and I thought my Dad would die. Worse, it was the last night of the movie and they already had the next movie in BIG LETTER on the sign above us, it was "The Last Tango in Paris". At that time, a very restricted movie and they had the large black panther on the sign and the XXX. My Dad had to stand under that sign. Ouch. Worse, when we got into the movie, before we saw our movie, we got the trailer for The Last Tango in Paris. I thought he was going to die, and me too.

14: This church is DROWNING PEOPLE ! Call the police.

Attending a Baptist church in the 50's I was brought up on the old "fire and brimstone" preaching, "**Repent or burn in hell**" . I often say I was saved from Hell when I was 5 but was born spiritually when I was 40.

A funny story back to the old Mission Baptist church. Of course being Baptist they had lots of baptisms. They had a baptismal tank up on the stage just to the right. When someone was baptized, after they dunked them under the water we would sing a song like "up from the grave He arose". They would then pull the curtains before they came up from under the water so that you wouldn't see something you shouldn't see as the baptized people wore thin white gowns and came up wet.

I was about 5 years old and all I heard was, "**does anyone else want to come and be baptized at this time, to die with Christ.**" What I saw was they would dunk the people under the water, pulling the curtain and I never saw them come up. I thought they were drowning them, dying for Christ and sending them to heaven. I couldn't believe it, **they were killing people**! What kind of cult had my Father brought me into? The police station was just across the street and I wanted to run over and tell them but I was more afraid of my Dad.

This was my first lesson on how easy it is to misunderstand what is really happening. Needless to say, I did not volunteer to enter the waters of baptism at that time.   I was too young to die.

Take the time to explain things to your children.

I did get baptized by my pastor who was my brother Lloyd when I was 15 along with my nephews who were my age and friend Harry. More about them later.

15: LEADERSHIP, Greatest lesson I learned was in Grade One.

It was lunch hour in Grade One at the Mission City Elementary School. My favorite hour of school as my older brother Glen and our friend Ken and I would pretend to be riding our horses thru the trails in the woods and down into the gulley. We could be the Lone Ranger and Tonto or Zorro but our favorite show was the 26 Men. This was a TV show of 26 Texas Rangers going out to save the world.

I remember standing at the top of the long staircase talking to my two comrades and decided that if each of us would go out and get two extra guys and then each of them got two more, and so on... we could get our 26 men and we could live our dream. So we agreed that at recess tomorrow we would start asking with the plan of the following lunch hour to all meet at the top of the stairs.

As I recall, 26 men or so (boys from 6-9 years old actually) meet at the top of the stairs that next lunch hour. My heart was bounding with excitement as I told them what we would do. We headed out riding two abreast and for the next and very best half an hour went up and down my favorite trails, stopping occasionally to water our imaginary horses. **We were living the dream.** When the warning bell rang I gathered the troops together and agreed to meet at the same place at the top of the stairs again tomorrow for another awesome adventure.

The next day my brother Glen, our friend Ken and myself stood at the top of the stair after lunch, **ALONE.**

I realized then that if I was going to lead, I had to make sure everyone was involved, had some input and had a chance to be the lead horseman. They needed a chance to enjoy the day as much as I did and to live their dreams, or I would become:

The LEADER OF NONE !

Power of mulitipcation: If I disciplined one person for a year, then we both disciplined one other person each for a year, and so on, in 33 years, the whole world would be reached.

16: What happens in the BARN, doesn't necessarily stay in the BARN

This story I was not expecting or wanting to put in but without it the pieces of the overall journey cannot be fully understood. I said thru the good and bad so here goes.

Not sure of the age but I think I was 5 as it seems to me all the other older kids on the street except for me and the neighbor were home alone while all the older ones were in school. We didn't have kindergarten then so we played together. Not sure how it started or who initiated it but we started to play getting naked and then caressing each other.

I know most people will tell parents to start to talk to your children about sex when they start puberty or around the age of 11 or 12. All I know is I started when I was likely 5, and **I knew** what I was doing. Many men I talk to started at about the same age.

The endorphin rush to the brain was so exhilarating and as such, very addictive. We had to have more and more and just could not wait for the older kids to leave for school so we could act out.

Then one day, I guess it was a Pro-D day at school as our older siblings were home and we got caught in the old barn. They ran and told Mom and we said we were sorry, tears and the whole works. I think my parents had no idea what to do with it so it was never discussed. Actually, we were only sorry we got caught, as it seemed harmless to us but oh, what an awesome feeling to get that rush.

I never did get the sex talk from my Dad as I guess he figured I already knew far more than I should. It was also, as I would find out later, part of his legacy that had never been broken but rather hidden and not talked about or discussed. Too bad that is such a taboo. **Ignoring definitely does not help anyone and history was just to keep repeating itself.**

I did not do much better with the sex talk with my boys but I think it should be a natural conversation that we start right at the beginning. Somehow make it a natural but comfortable everyday type conversation.

Whew, glad that story is done **... yup, still in the old shame mode.** That was not the end of sexual exploration for me for it has continued to be a major part or maybe a major interrupter of my spiritual journey as the story continues.

It needs to be discussed, openly, honestly without embarrassment, shame or guilt, so that we can move on with the rest of our journey.

Story # 17: <u>TWELVE YEARS IN PRISON.</u>

I hated school, all my 12 years of prison. I hear stories of people who loved school and their favorite teachers and friends. Not me. I could not name you one teacher and didn't really have any friends, occasionally one or two but they did not last. I was small, normally the runt of my class, short, very skinny and seemed to have a target on my back for any bully trying to make a name for themselves. I had it timed to arrive at school as the last bell rang and how to get out the door and down the street before anyone else.

I normally didn't take the bus in grades 8-10 in Burnaby but ran thru the woods as the bus was a bully's haven. It was 4 km but I could run like the wind and not even get winded. I was so light and likely seriously ADHD so had, and still have, the energy of a dozen. I loved the adrenalin rush of the run.

Not complaining, I just made the best of it and moved on.

Funny add on, later in my life I would marry into a family who are all almost teachers. I love them anyway.

Story # 18:   YOUR CHOICE

A story goes like this and I have seen this too many times.
Twin boys are born to an alcoholic father.

1) One boy turns out an alcoholic and wasted life,
    he said,**"I watched my Father."**

2) The other boy never drank and is a great success,
    he said**, "I watched my Father."**

I have seen and heard so many stories as I worked with people,
especially men, who blame their fate on their Father. I talk to guys
in the recovery houses and it seems 100% had an abusive Father.

I have seen, and history records, some of the worst men come from
the best of circumstance and some of the greatest men have come
from the most devastating lives.

You can choose: Self pity or self determination.
You can choose: I watched my Heavenly Father.

19: CHURCH PEW, some humour **for the child in all of us.**

This is not a spiritual story but it did happen in church.

We were about 10 years old and a bunch of guys would sit together in church. The parents insisted we sit up front so we had to behave and they could keep an eye on us. The Pastor was going to say a prayer so he asked us all to bow our heads and close our eyes. Us boys sitting on those old wooden pews would bend way over so we could write notes to each other on the floor with no one seeing.

As I bent over too far I let a great big fart go. It echoed on the wooden pew. Then dead silence throughout the crowded church. My buddy beside me let out a short giggle, then the guy beside him burst out a giggle too, then we all burst into hilarious laughter and we could not stop.

My Dad, sitting a few rows back came over and escorted us all, laughing so hard we were crying , out of the church. If I only knew it was that easy to skip church.

I can't remember what happened afterwards but I am sure my Dad and his belt had something to say, after all it was the 50's and that is not how you behaved in church. I am still careful not to bend over too far when in church, you never know.

He who farts in church, sits in own pew.

I commented that this was not a spiritual journey story but that is wrong. We are Spiritual Beings and everything is part of our journey whether it is in church, at home, at work, on vacation or in our leisure time. It is all our spiritual journey.

Story # 20: 5 x 0=5, PEER PRESSURE

The best thing I learned in school was not to be afraid to have my own opinion and not follow peer pressure. In Grade 5, the teacher asked:

"What is 5 times 0 ?"   Louise, my first big crush, said, "5".

The teacher asked by a show of hands, "how many agreed with her." Everyone in the class, but me, put up their hands. I really thought of raising my hand just to agree with Louise, to be on her good side, but I didn't. She probably still hadn't forgiven me for stealing that kiss in Grade 2 anyway.

The teacher turned to me and said, "Deryl, everyone but you believes the answer is 5. Living in a democratic country with 39 out of 40 voting for 5, 5 should be right. What do you think it is.?"   I said I don't know but 5 times 1 = 5 so I can't see 5 times 0 being 5, but I don't know...

When he said I was right, the answer is "zero", my confidence to stand by my convictions and to seek the truth, no matter if I was all alone, was created.

Seek the truth, not what others or even everyone else is saying.

(I am still working on not becoming too arrogant about it though that is a little harder for me being of a proud German heritage.)

Story # 21: MY IMAGINARY FRIEND, HEATHER.

I loved the woods or the bush, always have. In Mission there was a great forest right behind our house. It was likely about a couple of square blocks, but to me, it was greater than adventure land in Disneyland.

My nick name growing up was " Bush" and I am not sure how I got it but can only assume someone would ask where Deryl was and they would say, " in the bush" which was said so many times that it was just shortened to "Bush". I need to ask my brothers that question some day.

I must add that I did have one good friend. **My imaginary friend, I called her Heather**. I think I made her female as I have 7 older bothers, oops I mean brothers, and never had a sister.

I would talk with her as I walked thru the forests and we chatted about the trees, flowers, played in the creeks and admired GOD's creation. **Sometimes I wonder if that was really GOD** and I just didn't know it. GOD says we need to be like little children and have that simple faith of just accepting HIM as our friend.

Sometimes we just make it all to complicated.

Story # 22: CAREER CHANGE FLIP FLOP

My lack of love for school and non focus because of the bullies or my ADHD did not do me well. I just squeaked by each year into the next grade until Grade 12. They held me back in Grade 11 as there was no way for me to get enough points to graduate. I had good marks in Grade 12 math and sciences but failed French 10 about three times.

French was my "horse around" class. I ended up having to taking French in night school the year after I was supposed to graduate to get my French 10. They said the grades did not matter that much and all I had to do was just have over 80% attendance and they would give me my diploma and then I could move on with the rest of my life.

I could have done better if I would have applied myself, had a goal or a focus. My only goal was to survive the day to get home and play. I could have done some team sports but I sucked at sports back then and was always last to be picked. My older brothers were all stars in something so I could not followed them as the expectation for me was too high, **so I just took a different path.**

I didn't write this for you to feel sorry for me or to think that I had a deprived childhood. I didn't. **My childhood was AWESOME**, but that is because I normally only focus on the time after school when I had been let out. I was in the bush, building tree forts, hiking, climbing trees and building dams and I still am doing that today with my Grandkids. Also, I did have some good friends after school but it seemed everywhere I lived my friends did not attend the same school as me. Most came from the church we attended.

Sometimes I wonder if all that craziness of not passing Grade 12 and moving on was a GOD timing thing. You see, if I would have graduated, I would have become a draftsman. I had job offers to work on survey crews with Hydro, Tel and BC Rail. The BC Rail one really interested me as I love trains and we were going to survey the rail line from Prince George to some place way up north but I needed my Grade 12 so had to wait out the night school time. During that time I worked for my Dad in construction. We were building a school in Langley where I apprenticed with my older brother **Lloyd.**

The other career path I thought of was a Preacher. Three of my brothers were in the ministry and the other four in construction. My Dad was a "lay minister" (means not his fulltime job) and my grandfather was too. I just didn't feel the call. When I finally got my graduation diploma, I was waiting for a call from one of the drafting careers.

My brother Glen had joined the bank. Then they were going to transfer him to Dawson City, Yukon and he refused to go. I said really, that sounds awesome, what an adventure. They pay your way, you have a job, flights out and a northern living allowance. My brother quit the bank as he did get the call to become a Pastor.

I abandoned my ideas of being a pastor or a draftsman and ran down to the bank and said, "**Hey, I'll go to Dawson City,** all you have to do is change the first name on your files from Glen to Deryl". (OK, I was not to business smart). They couldn't do that, but loved my enthusiasm and were looking for people who were willing to move anywhere.

I joined the bank and got married in 1970 and we lived in Coquitlam, Golden, Vancouver, Kitimat, Prince George, Victoria, Prince George, Comox, Greenwood, Invermere, Oyosoos, Kelowna, Courtenay and then Gibsons. In Gibsons, Gwen and I agreed that we were done moving so I left the bank and we moved to Kamloops for 8 years and then moved to Kelowna in 2007 where we remain.

I worked for five different companies and was fired two or three times but always rehired, downsized twice and quit at least three times. **I did not learn to play the political game with upper management** and stood up for what I thought was right. It was not so much if I was right or wrong but rather my **arrogant attitude** of I knew better than anyone that caused my self imposed problems.

Also, in that this book is on "my spiritual journey", I am thinking many would think I spent years studying or in academia, not true, I have no post secondary education and most of the time I would sooner be playing in the bush than reading a book or even the Bible.
  My education has come from life, my experiences and my direct interaction with GOD.
I did not allow too much editing of this book as I want my Grandkids to hear me as they read this as they know Grandpa's English and what he does, they call it "Grandpa style".

I say this so you know where I come from. Academia is great for some, but I see GOD sometimes prefers to use the weak so that HIS glory can shine thru.

I like to think that is why GOD chose me to have such an amazing relationship with and to be given this opportunity to write about it honestly. The good and bad. I pray it will encourage you on your journey.

Being right does not give you the right not to be loving and considerate.

Allow others to live their dreams on their journey as well.

 Quick Story: I did 3 years in French 10, with the same teacher, it was my horse around class. My Mom & Dad managed an apartment after Dad retired and one day I came home and saw my French teacher standing at my front door talking to my Mom. I thought I was dead or at least " busted".

He grinned at me with a smirk, I know where you live and know your Mom… He was looking for an apartment to rent and ended up living right above us. I cooled my Tom Foolery in his class but still didn't pass.

THE TEEN YEARS at CAMP

23: SPRING CAMP, the story movies are made of:

1968, I am 16 and going to Spring Break Camp.

I was at church at the Easter service with all my buddies and found
out they were all heading out to camp for Spring Break. They all
went to school together in Surrey but I lived in North Burnaby so
missed out on that conversation. But I wanted to go.   The bus was
leaving right now for Hope Bay Bible Camp on the Gulf Islands. We
had no time to go all the way home to Burnaby and pack so the guys
said I could borrow their clothes. **In a few seconds** from nothing to
do that Spring Break to jumping on the bus with my buddies for
the **greatest life changing event of my life.**

There were 8 or so of us 16 year old boys on a ferry going to Pender
Island for a SPRING BREAK for one week at a mixed boy and girl
camp on an island…. **the thing movies are made of.**

(As I am editing this section in 2017 I am on that same ferry passing
by Pender Island)

We got off the bus at the camp and were set free to lay claim to our
cabin. The boys cabins were on the left and the girls were just over
the creek. I saw the furthest cabin in the woods and we all ran and
claimed it. Our counselor was a very gentle quiet man, likely about
20 years old. He took us guys under his wing and became like our
"big brother". After camp he invited us over to his place for sleep
overs, movies and great bonding as a group of young teens. Well, at
least until he was **put in jail for being a pedophile.** But that's
another story.

It was obvious to me from the start that whoever was running this
camp, my counselor I believe, really didn't have a firm grip on the
leadership, so I took charge. They had a volleyball game going on in
the field so I brought in water balloons and threw out the volleyballs
and made it a riot.

Darlene Wowoda, she put the sweet in SWEET 16 and put the Wow in Wowoda. She stole my heart before I got off the bus. She told me she was a Russian Princess but her family had been exiled, I believed her. **I would have believed anything she said.** Problem was I had fallen totally in love with her but she had a crush on my nephew Blake, one of our group. He is only a few months younger than me and looked like some Greek god with his long curly hair. Blake liked someone else and so on. The week camp had turned into a regular Peyton Place.

There was a creek that divided the camp, **the other side was the girl's side,** no boys allowed. Um... we were not going to let a little creek divide us. One night I found a big rope under a shed and snuck it to our cabin. I told the guys we were all to be good and go to bed very quietly, not like the precious 3:00 am stuff. Told them once the counselor was asleep in his cot we would tie him to his bed and then take him tied to his bed into the middle of the field, and then we would go and raid the girl's cabins. Everyone was in. **It was a blast. Can 16 year old girls ever scream loud.**

The next morning, Dave Griffin showed up, he was the head director for the Canadian Sunday School Mission (CSSM) who owned the camp. They set our Counselor free who was tied to his bed and then sent someone to come and get just me. **He said that Mr. Griffin wanted to talk to me.** My 16 year old male hormones and foolishness were being called on. I was in so much trouble. Then I remembered that Mr. Griffin and my Dad were good friends. Could this get any worse? I figured they would put me in the gallows and Darlene would throw rotten tomatoes at me in front of everyone and then send the picture to my Dad. I would be banned from camp forever.

I was doomed.

Mr. Griffin met me in his office and got up and shook my hand. "Deryl, has anyone ever told you that you have great leadership skills and creative talent?" I was thinking this was a set up and my Dad would come around the corner with his belt. "No, I said". "You do" he continued, " Deryl, I talked to your Dad and I would like to **offer you a job here at the camp** this summer to be our Camp Sport and Event coordinator."
WHAT ???

What a brilliant man. He takes this kid that has totally taken over his camp and got all the kids doing what he says, not the counselors, and decided the best place for this person is to get him on his side and channel all the energy and passion for good. I asked, "you want me to come to camp, run the games and stuff and you will pay me ?

I AM IN!!!

I never caused Dave Griffin or the leadership another ounce of trouble but I jumped on board and poured all my energy into helping them in any way I could.

If you try and work on someone's faults, you can maybe make them normal. If you try and work on someone's talents, they will soar.

Help build confidence.

24: "GOD PLEASE !!!" I screamed as Cal gasped for his last breath. In 1968

This journey started two months before that plea to GOD. It starts at Pender Island as we prepared to start Hope Bay Bible Camp's summer camps. There was a giant fir tree just behind my cabin where I would sneak out at 5:00 am to talk to GOD. GOD said that one day **I would have a place like this, where games with the young and young at heart could play and relationships be built.**

I was 16 and received that promise when I was 60. Not that GOD is slow in providing HIS promise but I was slow in being ready to take it on. Had I chosen a different path I am sure I could have been in charge of that camp on Pender Island, most likely I would have taken over the leadership from Dave Griffin when he retired as camp director. But I chose a different path, the path that led me the longer route to where I am today, living on that promise and even better at **"The Rock"**.

We did camp on Pender for all of July with new kids every week. One break between camps we threw some hay in the back of an old smoke belching pickup truck and jumped into the back. We did a full tour of all the tourist sites in Victoria from the back of a pickup tossing hay at the cars behind us. You would never do that today with a half a dozen 16 year olds. It was awesome.

The next camp was at Cecil Lake some 25 miles East of Fort St. John in northern BC. I rode with the crew up to Prince George to Ness Lake Bible Camp. Stayed overnight and did the big Tarzan swing and then Dave asked if I would take the bus to Ft St John where they would meet me as he had more stuff to put in the car. Sure, never been on a bus. For that matter I had never been out of the Vancouver area without my parents. For me to go by bus alone to the far northern frontier was an exciting adventure.

(Yeah right City boy, hang on)

I arrived at the bus depot in Ft St John very early in the morning and as Dave had instructed me I went into the diner. It was a classic 50's type diner. I sat down and ordered my breakfast.

A couple of local boys, men actually, drunk men to be precise, drunk at 6:00 am none the less were "chatting" loudly in the booth next to me. Their chat turned into shouting and shouting into an old fashion western brawl. They rolled over the counter and onto my table sending my coffee and breakfast all over the floor. I jumped up, paid the bill at the front desk and waited for the team outside. My first experience as a kid with the northern Wild West culture of the 60's.

Dave and the rest of the team showed up and we headed east of town about 25 miles to Cecil Lake where we were going to set up a camp from scratch on a farmer's acreage. **It was a rough country dirt road** but when we got to the valley where the Beaton River is we had to go down to the bottom of the valley and across the old bridge. This section was under road construction. Unlike today, then you would just drive beside the working equipment as they built the road and you found your way around rocks, boulders and trenches. Cal, who was 16 as well, and I got out of the car so there was less weight to bottom out. We would walk in front removing rocks and trying to make a leveler path for the car and trailer. It took a long time and at one point **a rock did hit the gas tank and gas started to leak out**. What could we do with no gas station for miles and we had a punctured hole in our gas tank.

I had a big wad of gum I was chewing in my mouth so I took it out, crawled under the car and jammed it into the hole. It worked. At least long enough to get us to the farm where the farmer could fix and provide us with gas.

The camp was out in a large hilly field covered in waist high grass and full of beautiful white birch. We set up a big old circus tent for the chapel and dining room then each of us set up an army tent at our hand picked location for us and our kids.

We had a problem... hornets or wasps, seemed like thousands of them. So Cal and I volunteered to head out to destroy all the nests in the trees in the surrounding area before the kids got there. Ok, you have two 16 yr old city boys in shorts and t-shirts, given a torch, a lighter and some shovels, heading into a forest in a dry August with the ground covered by waist high dry grass. **Do I really need to ask was anyone thinking here ???**

We created an extra long pole for the torch and went at it. Very surprised that there was no grass fire or at least not one we did not bang out by hitting with our shovels and wet gunny sacks. We destroyed likely 20-30 large wasps' nests. Needless to say, **some of the wasps got their revenge.** It became a badge of honor between Cal and I who had the most stings, without flinching. We were at 22 each last count.

Dinner was called, pancakes. Cal and I had an eating contest, we agreed we needed to eat one pancake for each wasp sting we had. Shortly after supper Cal had disappeared and I went looking for him as we had work to do. I found him in his tent but I could hardly recognize him. **He had turned allergic to the stings and his throat and face were swollen like in some horror movie.**

Dave and the camp nurse Doreen came running when they heard my scream for help. We were out in the middle of nowhere and needed to get him to the Ft St John hospital for a shot immediately. It took us likely an hour to drive out to the camp because of the road, especially with the construction, but now it was nearly dark and we only had minutes, not an hour. Dave and Doreen jumped into the front seat and we laid Cal in the back seat. I knelt on the floor in the back seat of the old Valiant car with a bucket of cold water and towels to try and control the swelling. The rest of the camp stayed back and prayed.

Dave drove as fast as he could but when we came to the construction area it looked like we had run out of time. All the cold water towels I could put on Cal were not working and his breathing was getting very laboured. I had been told that the threat was the swelling on his throat would close off his throat and he would chock to death without the Doctors shot. **Cal was now gasping for air and not finding it, he was pretty much unconscious**.

As the 16 year boy I was kneeing in the back seat. I realized we were just a minute or two away from **Cal dying so I just cried out: "GOD PLEASE !!!"**

Immediately, Cal sat up from laying on the seat. He pick up his pillow to smack me with it and said: "you got my pillow all wet!" **We stopped the car and just wept for joy and thanksgiving**.

Fifteen minutes later when we arrived at the doctors he examined Cal and said, "it is a miracle, he should be dead." Thank you Lord. As we were leaving the hospital Cal said to me. "Oh, by the way, just after supper I got stung again, gives me 23**.... I WIN...."**

When I left for summer camp my Mother made me promise I would not do anything foolish. During camp, we went back to that river as our swimming hole. Talk went on between the teen age guys and dares started that someone should try and swim across the river. We were in a quiet eddy but there was a good current on the other side. No one was foolish enough to try. I heard my Mother's **voice and promised GOD I would not do that**.

After the miraculous healing we were at the river in the quiet pool swimming and I guess that **sometimes the presence of GOD in my life is so overwhelming it is scary.** The thought of GOD caring about me. As an act of defiance and rebellion **and to take control back of my own destiny** and I think maybe to just be "normal" rather than a Child of Almighty GOD, I dove into the water and swam to the other side. THERE I DID IT !!!... I don't know why, but sometimes I just feel **I have to put GOD in HIS place**, or better said would be to put him (small "h") **where I am comfortable and controlling him.**

25: WILDERNESS CAMP, in 1968

The closest I think I will get to heaven while on this earth.

I was now 17 and going to my first real wilderness adventure. A one week backpacking hike into the peaks and valleys of the Rocky Mountains near Jasper, otherwise know to me as heaven.

(side note: Since my son was two we have tried to put the backpacks on and get out up into the alpine or woods at least once each year. Over forty year later and we are still doing it and now taking the Grandsons along, that is my son and two oldest Grandsons on the cover picture.)

I pretty much grew up a city boy but believed I was a mountain man inside. I always found a patch of woods to wander into but had never really gone into the wild, until then. I spent the summer working for the Canadian Sunday School Mission, now called One Hope Canada working in their camps. At the end of the summer they wanted to give a try in Wilderness Camping so offered all the workers that summer the opportunity to go and blaze the trail to see if it worked. We did, it did.

We left Vancouver and were hoping to get to the foot of the mountain that day. We were heading for small village in BC called Penny which is near Jasper. They were just building that stretch of road from the Jasper turnoff to Prince George so we would need to take a number of very interesting detours onto the logging roads. We were travelling along the Yellowhead highway just north of Clearwater when all of sudden, BANG…. We hit a big old cow that was on the road, it smashed the grill and damaged the car beyond driving. We hitched a ride back to Clearwater and got a tow truck driver to go get the car and see if he could fix it.

Luckily, or I should say, **thank you Lord, the Canadian Sunday School Mission had a camp in Clearwater**. It was late August so all camps were done so we stayed in the cabins. It was a beautiful camp right on the river.

The camp custodian was also the local Pastor and lived in a large old log house on the property. We were invited over for breakfast and had an awesome breakfast. **Not only was it very good but we were served by the Pastors two teenage daughters, Sharon and Gwen.**
  Four teenage boys being served by two teenage girls in a camp setting, you can imagine the flirting and joking that went on around that breakfast table.

Dave Griffin, our leader, acquired a vehicle and after breakfast we were on our way.

As a side note that teenage girl Gwen, I meet again at camp at Pender Bay Bible Camp the following summer and we would be married for almost 40 years. Funny how GOD brings people into our lives and has great plans for in the future but at the time, we are totally oblivious. HE was likely laughing thinking, if you only knew. Truth be told, I remembered Sharon and not Gwen, and Gwen remembered Cal and not me.

When GOD stops you in your tracks, pay attention.

26: UP INTO THE ALPINE MEADOWS, I call heaven.

We got to the base of the mountain where we met the rest to the crew and loaded up our packs and headed out. Just before we left, the cook mentioned that he had enough coffee but if anyone wanted sugar or cream, they would have to carry it. He showed what a week of sugar in coffee looked like, how much it weighed and cautioned us that we would carry our packs up 3,000 feet or more to base camp. Every ounce less on our back could make the difference of making it to the top or not.

Do NOT take excess baggage on your trip, but do not leave any essentials behind. A good life lesson too. Coffee yes, sugar no.

That day I converted from 2 lumps of sugar and milk in my coffee, to black. Not just black but Camp Black. You see, the cook had a big old pot that just stayed on the fire all week. It had a tea towel fastened around the top with clothes pegs and the towel that dipped just below the water surface. Once a day he threw a new hand full of coffee grounds into the tea towel, never removing the old, and that was our coffee. Coffee made in heaven after a long hike, especially the days it snowed. You had to sift the grounds out with your teeth.

Snowed? Yes, this was late August and we had almost daily snow squalls. I remember my first one well. We were sitting on the top of Mount Baldy just above base camp which was in the alpine valley. It was gorgeous on the top of that mountain and we looked in wonder at GOD's creation at the peaks, the glaciers and the valleys all around us.

We saw the storm coming in and our guide, an old mountain man type said, "Boys, find a big rock to crawl behind to get out of the wind because a summer blizzard is coming. Just stay put and do not try and take a single step as it will likely be your last". With that he pointed to where we were standing. A nice slope behind us to the base camp but a sheer thousand foot drop in front of us. Sure enough, within minutes we were in a blinding whiteout. He had told us it wouldn't last more than a few minutes so just wait out the storm. We did.

Life is like that to, sometimes your best choice is to just stay put and wait out the storm. (I have never really lived that though.)

It was awesome. The wind howled, the mountain views disappeared to the point you could not see your feet as we were in the clouds and blowing snow. We just huddled up behind this rock on the top of a mountain and listened. As quick as it came it was gone and there was only silence.

Everything was a blanket of white, even us. Slowly the view of the mountains peaks came back and then the glaciers and then the valleys came back into view. They were all covered in **pure white snow. A heavenly mountain top experience.**

We looked over the side to see a Grizzly bear and her cub making their way across the valley bottom. They had got caught in the storm too and were now quickly heading for home.

Back at base camp there was a glacier fed lake in the alpine forest. I couldn't resist and dove off the snow into the water. It was refreshing. Those who followed my foolery had other words for the glacierial water and for me for convincing them to join me by diving in.

The last night around the campfire in our alpine wilderness and under the star lit sky, we had a communion service. No matter how long I live I do not think that moment will ever be surpassed until I join Christ in heaven for that supper. I will not even try to describe it. The sharing, the honesty, the love, the forgiveness and the purity of that night. To have total communion with GOD at that high place, was heaven on earth.

God's Kingdom had come.

27: MEET MY WIFE to be at CAMP, "Get your own Broom!"

I arrived at camp this second summer at Hope Bay Bible Camp where I was to be the sports co-ordinator for another great summer.

We were there about a week before the kids were to come and we needed to set up camp. A great team, my nephew Blake (Lloyd's son) came along this year, my cousin Tim, Darlene was back and working in the kitchen, (oh yeah) **, Stan Porritt (would become a lifelong friend) and a Gwen Young**. The same girl that had served us breakfast in Clearwater after we hit the cow, and Ernie, who was going to be Gwen's camp boyfriend.

The first assignment I got was to set up the cook's tent. Oh yeah, I was going to set up the tent for the love of my life, Darlene. Dave assigned Gwen to help me, why … only GOD knows for sure.

Anyway, the relationship between Gwen and I went downhill very fast. She definitely was NOT going to be taking any orders from a boy, especially a Mennonite type German boy with a chauvinistic attitude. I figured she was just some diva princess who had been sent to camp.

We found a nice location close to the kitchen and I dragged the old canvas army tent over that way. The ground had a lot of pinecones and needles on the ground which we needed to clear so I asked Gwen to go to the kitchen and get the broom.

"Get your own broom!" She said with much attitude, which started our 40 year love affair. People used to say to us, you two fighting is just foreplay.

I looked at her and realized her Royal Highness was not moving off her spot. She hadn't done a thing yet so I went and got the broom, cleaned the area where we were to put the tent, moved the tent in place while she stood there arms crossed and looked disgusted with me.   So I asked her if she would be so kind as to at least hold the center pole up while I secured the lines of the tent.
 She agreed and went inside the old canvas tent which with no ropes attached so it wrapped itself around her. Did I mention it was in the sun and it was a nice hot summer day?
I told her I need to go get some pegs for the ropes and left for the kitchen. I called Blake, Tim and Ernie to come and watch, **"Let's see how long she survives in that sweltering hot stinky army tent before she quits"** and all the teenage boys sat down on the chairs, drank their coffee and watched and waiting with great amusement. I can still see that look on her face when she came out and saw all of us boys sitting there watching her and laughing.

The kids started coming every Saturday and we sent them home on Saturday with a new batch of them on Sunday.

One weekend between camps we were all doing laundry, hand laundry. I found some old green twine and put it up as a clothes line between the trees so we could hang our cloths over it to dry. We had to double our clothes over the green twine as we had no clothes pegs. When they dried, we had a new camp councilor uniform, all our clothes had a green strip across the middle. I thought it looked great but the girls were not impressed with their green lined skirts, pants and blouses.

The romance of the camp councillors was very interesting. Deryl loved Darlene but Darlene loved Blake, Blake didn't care. Also, Gwen and Ernie were a real item, then one day near the end of camp, Ernie told Gwen that he believed GOD did not want them to be a couple and he broke up with her.   Darlene made it clear to me that she had NO interest in me either, so Gwen and I spent some time together as jilted lovers.

After about 5 weeks of camp we were heading on the ferry back to the mainland and up to 100 Mile House where we set up a **new camp, now called Lake of Woods.** While on the ferry I was sitting in the back outside. Gwen and one of the 20 some year old jocks were talking. They got into a heated discussion about something and Gwen really held her own against him. I watched and fell in love with that girl at that time. The passion and energy she used to argue something with this guy really impressed me. It was likely over him being chauvinistic and her defending that she could do anything he could do and likely better. I am sure she could have.

Lake of the Woods was interesting as it was just bush when we arrived. We had to cut our way in with a chainsaw and machetes to make the trail, then build the plywood decks for the tent cabins, tent kitchen and eating area as well as chapel. We also built a dock on the lake for swimming and that was also our water source.

We would take two 5 gallon pails to the end of the dock, scoop up the water, then run it through a tea towel over a barrel to filter and adding chlorine to purify. One day my cousin Tim was just putting the big 5 gallon buckets into the water. He was bent over and just too tempting for me to resist. I gave him a "little" push and into the water he went, laughing as we all were.

Problem was he did not let go of the buckets which were full of water and by holding onto two buckets he could not swim or tread water and down he went. He finally let the buckets go which we later retrieved by diving and looping a rope to the handles. Oh, the craziness of being a teen. Mind you, I am now 65 and if that opportunity arose again, I would give my cousin just enough nudge to put him off balance and into the drink (literally) again.

When we left Lake of the Woods, I told Gwen if she was ever in Vancouver to give me a call and I would give her the royal tour. After all, that is what my Dad did to everyone who visited us from the prairies, so I knew all the best places. Our legacy.

On the Labour Day weekend Gwen did give me a call. She was staying at her brothers in Vancouver until she would catch the train to go to school at Briercrest Bible College in Saskatchewan.

Her "bother" was driving her crazy and she needed to get out, so I agreed. We did a walk around the Stanley Park seawall and caught up on everything. Started at English Bay and by the time we got to the 9 o'clock gun, which is cannon they fire off every night in Vancouver at nine o'clock, we were madly in love. The 9 o'clock gun became "our place".

That feeling that the sky is bluer, the grass greener and that you just glide above the sidewalk as you walk together, a little thing called love.

Great fun at the PNE and then she had to catch a train to go to school.

We wrote every day. It is hard for an 18 year old to stay in a romance when separated by a thousand or more miles, but the letters helped us to really get to know each other. I agreed that I would take the train out and come to the big weekend festival Briercrest had every year near the end of February called Youth Quake.

28: YOUNG LOVE, SWEET 16 on a moonlit night on a train.

This is another story I did not want to write, but if I am going to share my story I need show what a jerk I am too, and maybe help you not to be.

I caught the train in Vancouver and was heading to Saskatchewan in February. Who does that? Leave above freezing weather to go to minus 40 degrees. Now that was Fahrenheit back then but -40 in Fahrenheit and Celsius are exactly the same, C-O-L-D. That was before Global Warming… oh, don't go there.

I love, love, love trains and had never been on one so this was exciting. Also, I had never really gone out on an adventure of my own without my parents, brothers or camp crew.   It was night time so not much to see and I connected with a couple of young guys.   I could tell right away by their language and stories that they were not going to Briercrest Bible College's weekend youth rally so I kept that to myself.

They started to play poker. Now being a good Baptist boy I had no clue how to play cards. My Dad would not allow cards in the house. He even had a problem with Monopoly as it had cards in it. This was because of his gambling problems and where it had lead him until the meeting with the Angels we talked about earlier.

I had pretty much lost most of my spending money when the guys told me to look behind me. I looked and I was sitting by the window of the train at night which was the equivalent of a big mirror. These guys had been able to see my cards all along and that taught me a good lesson. I am just not sure what the lesson was.

This young girl walked by and they made some rude comments and after she had left said a few things about what they would like to do with her which offended me.   I decided to get up and leave. I wandered up to the observation car which was a glass dome above the regular passenger car. It was about midnight and no one was up there except one person, sitting at the front.   I wandered up and it was that girl.

I went over and apologized to her for the behavior of the other guys and told her I was not with them. We got chatting and she told me that now that it was past mid-night it was her 16th birthday. Wow, how nice. Well, one thing led to another and being alone **under the moonlit train car dome sky we started kissing….**

After we cooled off and she snuggled in, she mentioned she was on her way to a youth retreat at Briercrest. I died. Oh NO! what had I done. **I had to confess.** I said I was too, but that I was going there to spend the rally with my …uh… my girlfriend… ouch.

It was a great youth rally. Gwen showed me around and introduced me to all her friends. We snuck into her dormitory and she showed me her room. Her room mate was there and she introduced me to her, **this is "Patricia".** We said hi. How was I to know that in 40 plus years Patricia was going to be the love of my life and wife. The next summer, Gwen moved to Vancouver and we dated and were married on Dec 12, 1970.

Patricia was taking her college courses to be a Lab Technologist in Vancouver and would occasionally come over. After a few visits, Gwen felt I was flirting a little too much with Patricia and cut off that relationship for another 40 years. (More later)

Back to the girl on the train. During the spring when Gwen was still in Bible School and I was in Grade 12 at North Van High, in one of her letters she broke up with me. Said she had found a new guy skating. Well, I was tired of this long distance romance and if she came back to Clearwater where her parents lived, that was a long ways from Vancouver to date. So I rebounded and called the girl on the train and asked her out on a date. The silly girl agreed.

I had to hitchhike out from North Vancouver to Abbotsford but I could do it in about the same time anyone else could drive it. I used to find a perfect spot to hitchhike from and I would run with my thumb out. I was 130 pounds and no threat to anyone. One day I did 17 different rides to Abbottsford and back, about 150 km, but it wasn't as far back then as it was only 90 miles in the 60's. ha ha.

Well, that lasted a few dates and then Gwen gave me a call. She was at her brothers place in Vernon and invited me up for the May long weekend. Her brother Bert could drive me as he was doing college in Vancouver and heading to Vernon for the weekend to see his girlfriend.

Bert was about 15 years older than us and originally a pastor. He married the sister of Dave Griffin that camp Director I used to work for. He was pastoring in Merritt and ended up getting a divorce and leaving the ministry.

I remember another story about Bert. Bert married again to Olive and he was attending a church. Everyone there agreed he would be perfect for some church leadership. He had to decline because he was divorced and was not allowed to service in leadership at that church. What a waste of good talent.

Back to the weekend in Vernon. When I showed up Gwen and I pretty much had the place to ourselves all weekend. She asked what I had been up to since we split up and if there was anyone else? Well, I knew I couldn't lie as she could smell a lie a mile away. So I fesses up, but then she had broken up with me, what was I to do, sit around and cry.

Anyway, she convinced me not to go to the train girls track and field day at school which I had planned to do the following week. Rather, I wrote her a "dear John or dear Jane" letter. Whoos. **I have regretted that I was not man enough to go tell her in person all my life**. Gwen was very smart though. She figured that if I went to that Field Day, the other girl would likely win by convincing me to stay with her. After all, she was a good Mennonite girl, my heritage and Gwen was very British.

After Gwen died and I meet Patricia again some 40 years later, I asked Patricia if she knew that girl on the train as they were about the same age and had grown up in the same town. She didn't really know her except she did know that she was good friends with her sister. She had married and had kids. I really wanted to just go meet her and apologize for being such a young JERK.

I had just begun dating Patricia and didn't want to disrupt that relationship so I let it slide. That is my feeble excuse anyway.

Shortly later I heard she got cancer and died. I am not sure if my apologizing to her would have made anything better, but the fact is, whatever we do in life, right or wrong, has consequences we need to live with.

I have never been able to forgive myself for breaking the heart of the sweet 16 year old birthday girl on the train. I had NO business kissing anyway as I was already in a relationship. I should have stayed away from trouble on that moonlit night on a train. **My Dad said after his experience; don't put yourself in a situation you cannot stop.**

All choices have consequences.

29: My 1st Car, Suzy and 7 accidents in 1 year. In 1968

When I was 17 I got my first car, a VW bug for a $1,000. I remember my Dad dropping me off on Broadway and after the deal was done he left in his car and left me to drive my new, OK used 1966 VW bug home alone. First of all, it was a standard and I had driven my Dad's automatic. I pulled out of the sales lot onto Broadway or should say bunny hopped the car and realized I had no idea on how to get home to North Vancouver. I had been in the car with my Dad as driver and had driven that many times but I did not pay that much attention to the exact directions.

In life sometimes we just act like a passenger and don't really know our way.

I did know that I had to go towards Grouse Mountain and cross one of the bridges so I just kept heading north until after a very long process, I was home. Sure would pay to have and follow proper instructions or ask for details.

In the first year of driving in Vancouver I had 7 accidents. First one I was driving over Lions Gate Bridge and looking over at the water and boats not realizing the traffic in front of me had come to a stop. Ouch.

Next I was driving on a dark and rainy night on Hastings when a guy in a Jaguar slammed on his breaks to stop for a dog. I hit my brakes and did not have the stopping power of the Jaguar. I slid and slid on my bald tires in a very light car right into his rear. Man, Jaguars are expensive to fix.

Next I was going on a date with Gwen to see a movie and my Dad warned that it was a terrible dark and rainy night and I should not go. I did anyway and t'boned a car in the parking lot. Next day I was taking my friend to show him the scene of the crime. When trying to cross the 4 or 6 lane road to enter the mall parking lot I panicked and back up instead. Didn't realize the guy behind me was following me that close.

The final accident I knew that journey all too well. They were the roads I travelled every day from my house in North Van to Gwen's apartments near Cambie & Broadway. I flew down Seymour Street as I knew the lights, screeched around the corner onto Pender and peddle to the metal to get in line with the next set of lights. Someone else going at the 90 degrees to me was coming down Granville in a Toyota chasing the light too. We hit nose to nose and then end to end and flew down the others street without touching our brakes. We all walked away without as much as a scratch, but both cars were totalled.

GOD was definitely looking after us. Had we been a split second faster or slower it would have been a T'bone and I with a VW having no real strength in the frame, we would have been dead both me and my bride.

It was a Sunday morning around 9:00 am as I was on my way to teach a Sunday School class and hardly a car on the road. The good thing was, GOD still had more things for me to do, so HE saved me.

I have kept my guardian angels extremely busy all my life. I am really looking forward to meeting them one day and thank them but I am just a little worried they might want to give me a swift boot in the butt for all the grief I caused them.

I was going to give up driving forever but rather I changed to a very conservative driver and have not had an accident since, which is 50 years and some years I drove over 80,000 km a year.

Seems to take me 7 times to get things right. I heard a preacher say the other day that "7"is GOD favorite number, it is the number o perfection. So it makes sense it takes me 7 times to do anything, to get it right.

30: HONEYMOON DOOR that would not open in 1970

Dec 12, 1970 Gwen and I married. We arrived at the Blue Horizon Hotel to start our honeymoon. This was a fancy hotel at the time in Vancouver. I paid an outrageous price of $20.00 for one night on the 9th floor and that was for a nice suite. I was making $3,600 a year at the time. You can do the math to compare to today.

Anyway, we arrived at the hotel with confetti all over us. I was 19 at the time and looked more like 12. I wanted to open the door for my blushing bride so I pulled on the main door to the lobby:

It didn't move,
I pushed... it didn't move.
Getting frustrated I pulled then pushed then pulled and pushed again.

A nice older man came up behind me, put his arm around my shoulder and said:

"Take it easy son, you have all night".

With that he slid the door open sideways.

31: I WAS THE FIRST AND LAST TOPLESS BANK TELLER

My 32 years working for various banks was a very…. volatile career. I had people tell me many times that I just didn't seem like the banker type, and I loved that.

I started in Burnaby at the Brentwood Shopping Center. The manager there decided to have Hawaiian days. Now back in 1970, the banks did not do that kind of thing, they were… banks. We decorated the branch with palm leaves and made his office into a grass hut. Air Canada opened a booth with a free flight to be won. They flew in fresh pineapples and pineapple juice every day.

Now, to top it all off, this was the era when topless lunch bars were just in style. The manager decided to have the first ever, in any bank, topless teller. He took out ads and the next thing you know we are all over the paper, everyone was talking about it. Head Office's phone was ringing with complaints off the wall and even Alan Fatheringham who wrote the Editorial for the Vancouver paper wrote, "relax people, think about it, the topless teller is going to be that new male teller they have". Which happened to be me.

Thank heavens they cancelled the topless teller idea, but I hold the title of, and likely only to ever be, the only Canadian Bank Topless Teller.

That was the start of my banking career.

32: LIVING IN THE ROCKIES in 1971

I got married and started that job in the bank. From the age of 20 to 40 I spent building my career with not much growth in my spiritual journey, but a needed detour. My first move with the bank was to Golden for a year in the beautiful Rocky Mountains.

We loved it. We roamed around Lake Louise, Banff and many trips down to Radium Hot Springs. My Father in law once told me that the best thing you can ever do is to move 500 miles away from your in-laws if you want your marriage to succeed. I took his advise as Golden was 502 miles from Vancouver.

Years later, I am not sure if that was such good advice. He gave that advice because of his life experiences. **His mother in law and him did NOT get along**. She felt he was not worthy of her only daughter as he was just a poor preacher. He was making less than a dollar a day back then and all the free farm chickens and eggs they could eat.

Strange, you would think that she would be the last to be prejudice of someone marrying beneath them. You see, she was born into nobility back in England. Then she fell in love with a commoner and married him. Her very wealthy and affluent family disowned her. If I recall correctly, they were Cartier's and originally from nobility in France.

She was pregnant very soon after the marriage and soon after that the husband came down with tuberculosis, which was very serious back then. He was put into a Sanitarium. He tried to see her and walked miles but was turned back. He died before their daughter was born. This was my wife Gwen's Grandmother and the baby was Gwen's Mother, Hilda.

With her husband deceased and shunned by her family she resorted to begging on the streets of London. I remember Gwen telling me she took her Nana to see the movie "Oliver", the story of a poor begging orphan in London. Nana slept through the movie. Gwen asked her why and she said: "why watch it, I lived it."

They moved to Winnipeg and started to attend the Salvation Army church because it was the Salvation Army that fed, clothed and got them moved and their new start in Canada. There she meets a very nice man who married her and took her daughter Hilda as his own. So they become Wharton's. Years later, Hilda, that is Gwen's Mom, met Robert Young and they married.

Now I knew both the Grandma, who we called Nana, though I don't know her real name, and Hilda for only a few years before they both passed on. For me, they were awesome and I had more fun playing games at Christmas time with them than ever. But Nana died a month after we were married and my mother in law, Hilda, died a year after we were married. More of that story later.

Amazing that even after you may have been treated so wrong, unless you take the action, the Legacy repeats itself.
Also interesting that Gwen and I married so young, but good thing as Gwen needed me when her mother and grandmother died shortly after we got married. She figured that if we would not have gotten married she would have likely looked after her Dad and likely never married or had children.

Back to our time in Golden. My brother and nephew were coming up for the July 1 long weekend and wanted a grand tour of the Rockies. We had about $5.00 in the bank and I had already taken the one and only pay advance available. Our cupboards were bare and there was no Visa or line of credit back then.

Gwen said we will just have to trust GOD to provide. The day they were to arrive we received a cheque for 2,000.00 in the mail from Nana's estate. We never expected anything. Keep in mind, I was making about 4,000.00 a year back then so that was half a years wages. Awesome and such timing. We would see a lot of that.

We had a great weekend.

GOD loves last second rescues.

33: HIPPY BANKING in 1972

From Golden we were transferred back to Vancouver and I worked just up the street from the Vancouver Sun and Province building at 8th & Granville. The post office went on strike and the welfare office was just across the street from us. This was 1972 in the height of hippy times and we were just off 4th Ave which was Hippy Haven.

The Welfare department advised us that they could not mail out the cheques so all the welfare people would need to come in and pick up their cheques at the welfare office and then they would come across the street to cash their cheque at our branch. We didn't have any electronic banking then so all was done by cash and cheque.   We staffed up for the big day. I had 12 teller lines fully running all day and even open extra hours.

The taxi's that brought people to the welfare office were lined up and down Granville Street and the welfare people totally filled the inside of the bank. We didn't have the single line and wait for next teller back then. It was line up behind a teller and hope your line was the fastest.   The line up went outside the bank and down the street for over two blocks and was three or four people wide.

I had over 20 tellers working as I could not close a single line.
 When someone was due for a break I just slotted another teller in and carried on, unheard of in the banking world back then, usually they would have to close and balance their cash and sell their cash to the next teller which meant counting it all, which could not happen. That would take a half an hour to do, forget the rules, we are under siege here and need to go to drastic measures. It turned out with the body odor, marijuana and smoke smell I needed to switch my tellers off in 20 minute intervals or they would get sick.

At one point, a very distinguished and very loud important client of ours walked in and was at the very back of the bank. It was Alan Fatheringham, yup, editorial of the topless teller guy from a previous story. He shouted out, **"THESE LINES ARE ABSOULTELY DISGUSTING. DO SOMETHING ABOUT IT!!!"**

I jumped up onto the counter, walked across the counter to the center of the bank stepping over the tellers and said, **" I AGREE, THESE LINES ARE TERRIBLE, CAN EVERYONE PLEASE LINE UP IN NICE STRAIGHT ROWS !!** " and I motioned with both my arms to form nice straight organized lines.

Everyone laughed and we all endured the rest of the day.

Now keep in mind, my Bank manger, my boss, was of the old school. He wore an old black suit and narrow tie and had a military type crew cut. He believed in the old bank rules. One day he sent me home to change as my pants were unacceptable. Go figure, Gwen had made them especially for me working down on Hippy Street. They were bright orange with about a one foot wide bell bottom, the top was an Elvis type ruffles shirt and a wide Hawaiian type tie. I looked really hip. Now can you imagine why he would have sent me home to change?

I was tempted to put on my white Beatles Sergeant Pepper suit, but refrained. Well, not that day anyway. I rode my bike to work back then and there were no bike lanes and we lived by Stanley Park so that took some time. I was in no hurry.

The manager let me run the zoo on welfare days but he had had enough of me and had me transferred to Kitimat, about as far away as you can get.

Maybe good to move 500 miles away from an irate boss too.

34:   KITIMAT, means "people of snow" BIG TIME !

The winter we were in Kitimat was likely their snowiest they ever had and I loved it. The snow was so high that our single story side of a duplex was encapseled in snow. I have a picture of the dog and I on the roof and it looks like we are in a snowy field, not the middle of a subdivision. All you can see are holes where smoke is coming out of chimneys.

On New Year's Eve, my Father in law, Reverent Robert Young, woke up in the middle of the night and woke us up. He always had premonitions and he said something was terribly wrong. I turned all the lights on as I respected his comments from past experiences. A funny smoke was coming out of the furnace, which was in a closest on the main floor as it was only a 900 square foot single story house on a slab.

We called in a repair man the next morning and he said: "wow, I can't believe you people are still alive." He said a brick had come loose from the ice and snow on the chimney and had fallen down blocking the chimney. The carbon monoxide was quickly filling the house just before I turned the furnace off. If we had not shut our furnace off when we did we would have all been dead.

In May, I finally put my sprinkler on my lawn to try and get rid of the snow.

On July 1st, half my staff at the bank left as their husbands who were RCMP or teachers got transfers out of town. For the next three months some of the staff and I would start at 4 am, do our work, then run the bank from 10-3, then do all the missing staff work till 10 pm. Slowly we found and trained new staff.

In October we got audited by the Bank. They found we had done all the essentials but the other work which is normally done and double checked was not. *I was dismissed.*

35: My 1st born... NOW I KNOW WHAT LOVE IS

During that time in Kitimat my wife was pregnant and we had our first born son. Gwen got toxemia and gained well over 100 pounds (I think) and was admitted to the hospital about 2 months before her due date. It was serious.   One month before due date they enduced and we waited for the baby's arrival. My son came a month early. He came before the July 1 disaster started at the bank, *thank heavens*. I remember going from work to the hospital, which was half way home and sitting with my wife, waiting, making sure all was well as could be.

Now we need to back up here. When I was a child growing up in church, we sang "Jesus loves me". We memorized and quoted John 3:16 a quad zillion times. Ok, maybe not that many. I grew to actually hate that verse. It was so overuse.   You can see it at ball games where someone has a sign and so on, give me a break people. **It became trite and meaningless to me.**

Back to the story, one night the Doctor came by and said: "The baby won't be here until morning, you might as well go home and get some sleep Deryl." I said, no, I would stay. At 2:00am I checked as Gwen was getting major contractions and I could see the top of the baby's head coming out. I ran into the empty and quiet hallway and screamed as loud as I could, **"THE BABY IS COMING, THE BABY IS COMING !!!!!"** Nurses flew into action from everywhere. They wheeled Gwen out and across the hall to the delivery room, seconds later, I heard him cry. One of the nurses brought my son out to me. He was looking at me with biggest brown eyes in total wonderment, like he was saying, "so this is life". I took him into my arm and wept.

I finally knew what GOD meant when HE said, "For God so loved the world that He gave His only son, that who ever believes in Him, shall not perish but will have eternal life." John 3:16, the most precious verse now for me in the Bible. Because finally, I knew what LOVE was. *To love so much that I would die for that person*.

I understood GOD's love.

36: Prince George 1 1974-1976

Meanwhile, back at work or better said, back at being dismissed and unemployed, I now had a wife and baby and needed employment. I advised head office of what had happened and I was re-instated on a probation period and would report to a branch in Prince George on Monday.

I was in Prince George about 12 months and did a very good job. My manager and I are still good friends today. Spruceland branch was what some called the hell hole of the bank. I had about 18 on staff and at one point, my most experienced teller had 3 months.

You see, after they learned cash, and were being paid almost minimum wage, they would get a job very easy at a union job in one of the grocery stores. Especially the store right next door. I used to have coffee with the managers over there and suggested I just change my sign into " Overwaitea Training Center ", they laughed.

The banks finally figured it out after all our requests and started to pay their staff better.

I had an Assistant as well, and after he left, I heard that he used to hire the tellers based on how well they were in bed. I remember one job posting we did and had 107 applicants, all young girls just out of school. None with experience or at least not in banking. If I would have known his hiring criteria I would have fired him. More of that type of characters were to come in my career with various companies and associations.

My re-actions would chart the destiny of my course and my reputation. To stand up for what is right is not always seen by the world as the right thing to do. What I called a champion for women's rights and against abuse, some saw as a threat to them and their privilege.

I suggested to the manager because we got along so well that when the Assistant Manager left, which was very soon, I would love the job. Luckily, he did not take me up on that but rather I got transferred to Victoria. Very nice.

We bought a house in Victoria built in 1902 which no one would buy as the basement always flooded. I looked at it and it had a 3 foot retaining wall by the road which was acting like a dam. The house was above that and a long sloping hill behind going up for miles. The basement was only about 6 inches under ground level. How could that be that it floods? So we bought it for a steal.

I dug what is called a French ditch around the house about 3 feet deep. Put in drain tile which drained out to the retaining wall and filled the ditch with drain rock. I put holes in the concrete front retaining wall to move the water off my property and the basement never flooded again.

We did this kind of thing a lot. We bought and sold 13 houses. When transferred in, we would find a fixer upper in a good neighbourhood, do the work and about 18 to 24 months later the bank would move us. The bank would buy my house for top appraised dollar and pay all the legal and realtor fees. I believe I made more money and tax free because it was our residence from buying and selling houses than I did working at the bank.

Gwen loved it as she was a very creative interior designer and could do an elegant job for pennies. She thrived on that with her Scottish heritage. Her Dad was Scottish, born in Edinburgh and moved to Winnipeg when he was a teen. He told me a story once that they were booked on the Titanic but someone got sick and they had to take another ship. Thank heavens.

I was only in Victoria for 9 months, just enough time for my 2nd son to be born.

37: GOD's HEALING POWER

When my youngest son, Chris, was born back in the mid 1970's the doctors told us he had a hole in his heart, or something like that. They advised that he would likely be quiet, inactive and slow because of it.

They recommended we wait until he was two and take a look into some type of heart operation. Being about 26 years old myself at the time this news was terrifying and upsetting because as his father, **I could do nothing to fix it.**

Because we had two little guys ages 2 and a new born we did not attend a church regularly at that time. We tried to attend the Alliance Church in Victoria but only went a few times. But for whatever reason they paid attention and cared about us. They would call occasionally to see if there was anything they could do and one day Gwen, in tears, told her concerns about our new baby and his heart situation.

One Sunday afternoon there was an unexpected knock on the door and two elderly gentlemen where standing there. Oh no I thought, Jehovah Witnesses. I opened the door to tell them we were not interested when they introduced themselves as "elders" from the Victoria Alliance Church which we had been to once or twice. They said they had heard our baby had a heart problem and asked **if they could come in and pray over him.** I thought, yes, no harm in that, I have read in the Bible that if any was sick among you, you were to call upon the Elders of the church and they would come and pray.

Sure, come on in and I showed them to the baby's room. Gwen came but I left. I was very skeptical. In a few minutes they were gone and never to be seen again as we moved back to Prince George shortly after.

At Chris's next check up the Doctor noted that he could hear no sign of the heart murmur or issue but we would keep an eye on it. Now if any of you know my son Chris, the very last thing he is is quiet or inactive or slow. Actually the very opposite and would likely be labeled extreme ADHD or whatever they call hyperactive these days. I just call it very energetic.

I write this today as in a few hours, (2015) six of us are meeting from our church to discuss appointing some "elders" to our new church plant. What I can see, a church elder is to care for those in their church family.

I never thanked those two men for taking the time out of their day and caring enough to even know we had that concern. Then more importantly their faith to do what GOD had called them to do, to care for others.

By doing so, God wondrously healed my son Chris and it changed our lives, amazingly.

38: MY FIRST AND LAST ACT at the COMEDY CLUB.

I was in Toronto on a two week course leaving my wife and little kids at home. I don't remember the course but I do remember the weekend.

There were likely about 40 of us guys at the course and as usual, **I was the class clown**. Always had a good joke or comeback that got a thousand laughs over the weeks seminars.   The guys all agreed that I should do the Amateur Comedy Night at the local pub in downtown Toronto on Friday night. They signed me up but the owner wanted to hear my stuff to screen me and they told him: "We are bringing 40 guys down to drink beer, if you want us, you put Deryl on stage, period". He did as Money talks. **He would regret that decision.**

I was brought up in a good Baptist family. No drinking, no gambling, no smoking etc, but I was far away in Toronto with "the boys" and was seeking adventure.   To clarify, these were guys from all over Canada and I did not know any of them before or would never see them again, so why not.

Friday night we started by bar hopping. I am not sure if I had ever had a beer before but I was going at it that night. Problem was I was drinking it like pop, not slowly and not eating anything. Well, we got to the comedy club and it was my turn. I got up on stage and said, "Helloooooooooooooo.... I am Derr——rryl " My 40 fans cheered wildly like it we had just won the Stanley Cup, banged their beer glasses on the table and started to chat, Derr-rryl, derrr-rryl. Derr-rryl in drunken slur.

This was the age of Pierre Trudeau and just after he introduced the special oil tax and Alberta and Ontario were in a big feud. Pierre did his fuddle duddle and the Albertans were saying " Let the eastern bastards freeze !".. So I figured I would endear myself to this Ontario crowd by starting off with "I am Derr-rryl and I am from the West…. Just came out here to see if you eastern bastards are freezing yet!!??? " …. The easterners stood up and were booing me big time, my 40 guys stood up and cheered loudly, chanting DERYL, DERYL, DERYL, banging their beer glasses on their tables all the louder.

The owner realized that he was seconds away from a full out brawl. Two big guys came out of nowhere, picked me up, one under each arm, **walked me out the back way off the stage** and opened the back emergency door with my head. They threw me into the alley which thank heavens had a snow bank. I jumped back up and ran for the door to get back in and finish my session, when my buddies met me and dragged me away saying, we better go elsewhere.

That was the ended of my career as a standup comedian.

I did not stick to the script we had written but went for the shock treatment, it worked. I got a lot of attention, none of it good and we did not accomplish what we set up to do. But got a great story !

39: THE GREATEST BLUFF OR GREATEST FOOL.

When we left the Comedy Club back when I was in Toronto, the boys put me in a cab and we headed for the next bar. We went in and quickly realized this was not just any bar, but a strip joint. Ooo-la-la…. Too many beer and my inhibitions were gone. We chanted thru a number of shows and then caught a cab back to the place we were staying. The poor cabbie had to stop at the side of the road while I threw up all that beer in my stomach onto the Toronto streets.

Luckily, one of the guys had taken me under his wing realizing that I had not been exposed to this type of life and he took me back to my bed before I got into any more trouble that I would have seriously regretted.

Thank you Lord for that guardian angel, whoever he was.

The next day we hung out at the hotel. My employer owned this hotel and used it to house staff attending seminars. The top floor was the executive lounge which was gorgeous. It had a great lounge area and a pool table.

That evening the guys started a large poker tournament. I had not played much poker and pretty much did not know what beat what, but I was "IN". I think it was penny poker but it soon graduated to nickels, dimes, quarters and then bills.

We had been playing for some time and the guys were growing tired of poker so we had one last game. I had an awesome hand. I had a straight flush, king high, so the only thing that could beat me was a royal flush. What are the odds? I kept upping the bet until there was just two of us left and the pot in the middle of the table looked like a mountain of money to me. I borrowed some money from my buddy beside me and went ALL IN. "Shut up or put up" I said to the last survivor. "Put your money where your mouth is or fold like a baby" I taunted. "Your bluffing" he said. "Me, I wouldn't know how to bluff if I wanted to". Most of the crowd agreed with that as they had seen me play and could not understand how I was still in the game. They all stood and watched in awe.

He folded.

I threw down my cards. (I know you don't have to show your cards in a situation like that, but I had to. I love that big James Bond type scene) But again, I had maybe too many beers as it was not exactly a straight flush. My eyes did not see well and some of the black spades were actually black clubs. Everyone said, "He was bluffing".

I looked down in amazement and thought " OH NO" but I stayed quiet and let them all think I was a Poker Guru but I knew **I was really just a Drunken Fool who got really lucky.**

My wife even today, some 40 years later, knows she can beat me at most things if she can get me to be cocky, because if I do, I usually do myself in.

I am my own worst enemy, but still love it.

40: Oh Crud the game of the JET PILOTS.

So Sunday night I asked the guys if they had ever played "Crud" on the pool table? Nope, no one had ever heard of it. I pretty much knew that as the game was created by the Snowbirds. Not the Canadians going south but the pilots of the Snowbird jets that do the aerial displays at your July 1st celebration. I hung out with those guys when I lived in Comox as they trained there in the spring.

Well, let me teach you. First of all, get rid of all the balls except the white and the black ball. Then put all your pools cues back on the rack, we don't need them. This is a hand ball and round robin game.
  Then as many guys as want to play set up around the table.

Now, the guy at one end throws the black ball and tries to make it rebound as many times as possible and get it into a hole. He has to hit at least one bank before going into a hole. If the black ball goes into a hole the guy holding the white ball is out. The next guy steps up. The white ball holders job is to throw the white ball with his hand and try and hit the black ball, if he hits it, he is still in and the next guy in line is to get the white ball in his hand, he must go to an end and from either end hit the black ball before it stops or drops into a hole. We go until the last man is standing.

We had a great and very wild time.   About an hour into the game, and likely about 2 am I was down to one player left. I still remember running like crazy to get that white ball then running to the end of the table and throwing it with all my might as the black was just passing in front of the far corner pocket. It jumped and skipped across the table, hit the black ball on a little bounce and just took off. It flew off the table and hit the middle of the great big plate glass window right in the middle. It crashed through the window with the pieces along with the ball flew out into space as we were on the about the twelfth floor. It went crashing to the sidewalk below.
  Thank heavens no one was there at 2 am.

In a matter of seconds all 40 or so of these bank managers, supposed responsible citizens and friends disappeared. I said, "Don't worry, I did it, I will take full responsibility." **But they had all disappeared in a flash and were in their beds pretending to be sleeping.**

Moments later, I heard the elevator door open and John, the manager of the building and someone I knew from when I worked at the Main Office in BC walked in. He had heard I was there, my comedy club scene, the taxi ride, the poker game". He looked around. I shrugged my shoulders and he said: **"Priebe, I should have known. "**

I was not invited back to Toronto for a long time.

I thought, Is all this really the reputation I want?

41: Prince George 2 1976-1978

We lived about 9 months in Victoria and I got a call from my old Bank Manager/Boss in Prince George. He said "Hey Deryl, you remember you said you would like to do my Assistant job when it became open, well, it is, and I would love to have you come back and run it for me."

I laughed and said, "Do you really think now that I am living in Victoria that there is any way I would come back way up north to Prince George again ?" I laughed some more and then hung up.

A little while later I got a call from Human Resources in Head Office. " Hi Deryl, we have 3 job offers for you, Fort Nelson, Fort St. John, or Prince George." I replied, "Prince George sounds great, when do you need me there?" He said, "Monday will be fine".

That is the way it used to work back then or the other option was I could have quit. I had a wife and two babies. We moved back to Prince George.

Many people of the generations after me complain about such treatment, but it was a different era then. We had just come out of two major World Wars and the world was still all run like the military. Authority spoke and you jumped. My generation being the baby boomers pushed back on that with things like the hippies, Martin Luther King type stuff and feminists movements.

We were in Prince George for about 18 months.   During that time, a good friend of mine and I had a standing bet as which one of us would be first to get our first branch managership.   One day I received a letter from the bank congratulating me as I had been appointed manager of the Stewart branch. I gasped, I got my dream job but in a nightmare location. What do I do, if I decline it's the unemployment line, if I accepted, I may never see the world again.

When we lived in Kitimat a few years before some friends of ours were doing some work up in Stewart for a few months. We decided to drive up and see them for the weekend. Problem was there really wasn't a road back then, they were kind of building it.

We had cheap little Datsun and loaded it up with supplies and headed out. At some points we were driving in streams, rutted logging roads and passing 4x4 with broken axles. We made it. The scenery was unbelievable. We drove over lava beds, along side of glaciers and high towering peaks. We even visited Hyder, Alaska. If you have been there, you know what we did, if haven't, don't worry about, you have not missed anything a trip back to the 1800's in the wild wild west saloon would not be.

A barge came in once a week to Stewart if the weather permitted. If you were not at the store that afternoon to get your bread, milk and whatever, you would have to beg and borrow from neighbors. They had a nurses station at the mine I think so any medicals were usually flown out. But the town sits under this towering peak with a glacier hanging over it located on the pacific coast just off the Alaska panhandle, north of Prince Rupert. Flying in or out days were limited.

I told the bank I had two babies and the youngest needed to go see the Doctor on a regular basis as he was born with a hole in his heart. Ok, I didn't think they would believe me if I told them some Christian Elders came and prayed over him and he was healed. I must confess, that would not help my story for not going to Stewart. Forgive me Lord.

We never heard back from the bank and waited for the other shoe to fall. A few days later I got a call from my friend. Ha, ha he said, I beat you. I got my 1st managership, I am going to be Manager of the Stewart branch. I fell to my knees and said quietly, "thank you Lord", then said congratulations to my friend and that **I would GLADLY buy him lunch.**

He moved to Stewart around Christmas and I believe the only employer up there, Grand Duke Mines, closed on New Year's day. What he moved into was families who were all of sudden going from extremely high paying jobs to nothing. They could not sell their houses as everyone was trying to sell and move out of town.

He ended up with all loans and mortgages in arrears and no fault of his, likely the most hated guy in a very small town.

I can state, he is actually a very nice and considerate guy, but he had the worst job at the worst time. He lost his marriage too. He left the bank some time later and has set up his own shop and the last time I had coffee with him, he was doing ok.

For me and my family, we missed that disaster by a hair. Instead, a few days after I got the call from my buddy, the bank called and offered me a job in Comox. Great I said, where is that ? On Vancouver Island, just north of Nanaimo.

You have to wonder if GOD had my friend go to Stewart for just a short time while we lived nearby in Kitimat for only 1 year, so I would go up and see that I would not move there when my dream promotion came up that would have been my nightmare. Also that my son had his medical condition which was likely the ONLY acceptable excuses the bank would have taken or they would have fired me for not going.

We went, and Comox has become where we call HOME.

42: THE WORLD STOPPED in 1981.

We lived in Comox from 1978 to1984. One of the longest places I have ever lived and it was good. We made the best life long friends who we still visit today, though we have moved all across the Canada.

Friendships are hard to get and when you do, you really need to work at keeping them. My friend Bruce and I have called each other to chat almost every Sunday and maybe catch a coffee or a sail in our boat once a decade. **Friends like that are hard to find and even harder to keep unless you make an effort.**

If you remember May 13, 1981, you know the rest of this story. That day Pope John Paul II was shot and nearly killed by a Turkish gunman from only 15 feet away **AND THE WORLD STOPPED.**

I am not Catholic but this incident caused the world to stop for a moment, and look around. The world changed forever. For you younger folk, it was like the Lehman Brothers crash in late 2008 and the world went into a tail spin. Now in 2017 the world is still throwing billions at economies and trying to get the system working again. World Governments have gotten so crazy that over many countries while I writing this have negative bond interest rates. I would have been locked up in an insane asylum had I suggested such a thing before 2008.

The world economics had the Baby Boomer phase from 1945 – 1981, 36 years. Growth, with interest rates going from 0.5% to 18% and high inflation. Then the next cycle went from 1981 to 2008, if you look at interest rates, you could take that to 2016, as interest rates started the first real sign of climbing in Dec 2016. That would be 36 years. Interest rates went from 18% to 0%. No guarantee on the accuracy of these numbers or any conclusions. It is just and observation.

In the late 70's until May 13, 1981, I was doing loans and mortgages. As we moved closer and closer to May 13, 1981 my appointments sky rocketed. I could not keep up as I was booked further and further ahead as inflation drove prices higher and people just wanted to buy "whatever" now, because they thought it would be much more expensive tomorrow.

Please note, it seems things go in cycles, some large cycles like interest rates, and some short. Some say the house market has a 7 year cycle. Seems pretty true to me and what I have observed in my life. The temptation is to buy high as it is the trend and greed; and sell low because of fear it is going lower. If you can figure out how to save your money when things are high to buy when low you will have mastered finance. Good luck ! It is a well known fact but very few succeed even when they know what will likely happen.

The Friday before the Pope got shot I was doing record numbers of loans and mortgages. Further to that, we were doing the largest amount of loans and mortgages of any branch in western Canada, we were considered the Golden Branch with my manager as the golden hair boy. We were the sales champion. I sold more VISA cards in the VISA campaign than anyone in Canada.

The week after the Pope was shot, when I returned to work and the market died. For me the market at the time was doing loans for logging, fishing, land development equipment, housing and car market, as that drove my loans and mortgages at the time. I don't think I wrote another new loan or mortgage until October and then only very few.

Interest rates had gone in a short time for mortgages from 10% to 18% and loans to 21% or 23%. Yet people were taking out maximum mortgages as they thought rates were going to 30% or higher.

Bond yields, the Govt of BC issued a 30 year bond paying 18%, government guaranteed, but the Government had to withdraw the offering as no one would buy it as they thought the rates would be going higher. Wow. I really wish I would have bought my Mom that 18% Goverment Guaranteed bond for 30 years. Who knew?

I remember stating that if mortgage rates EVER got back to a 5 year mortgage at a low 10%, I would lock in so fast. Everyone I said it to agreed and said that will never happen. Who would have never dreamt that mortgage rates would go down to 2% or lower? I heard of one European Bank where people who had a floating rate to prime actually had a negative interest rate mortgage. Wrap your head around how that works?

What happened is people stopped for a moment when the Pope was shot. **The momentum stopped.** The music stopped and everyone rushed to grab a chair as the game of musical chairs goes.

The world seems to continue to repeat with just different names. It seems to be the world "Legacy", **as fear and greed still seem to rule over common sense.**

Evil over good.

43: FORECLOSURE KING 1982

As the sales business had died the only work was doing collections. I volunteered to be the Special Debt officer. The Bank agreed and most sales people were glad to hand over all their bad loans and mortgages to me to get them off their books and responsibility. I ended up getting a large allotment of the loans in arrears for personal and businesses for the north part of Vancouver Island.

My life was with my lawyer on one side and my bailiff on the other. The bailiff loved his job. He was a big crazy man. His favorite story was once we went to reprocess a fishing boat and the fisherman pulled out a shot gun and laid it right on the bailiff's head. The bailiff said you better not miss, you are only getting one shot and then I am taking you down. He loved that stuff, scary.

I did not love it but when people asked how I could do it, I said, most of these people are really good people, who just got caught up in the wave of greed or timing. I go in, sit down at their kitchen table and lay out the options as honest as I can. 99% of the time they go for it, sometime they even give me hug and a few tears as it is finally all over and they can start again. The 1%, well, they ended up in the hospital from ulcers, insanity or suicide. They were pretty much all my friends. I would sooner then dealt with me than a stranger who didn't care about them.

I foreclosed on houses where they had cemented the basement drains and then turned on all the taps. The neighbors called when the water was coming out the windows. They would see how many walls they can throw a metal bar thru the gyproc or a boat with a big axe hole in the bottom of the hull sinking the boat and the moorage dock to the bottom of the harbour.

My boys asked me years later, why was it we could go down to the Comox wharf and play on all the boats and none of their friends could. I said because every Sunday I would take them down to the wharf while I checked all the boats we had reprocessed. We had taken over an entire closed off section of the harbour. One gorgeous hand crafted built boat cost more than 300,000 to build, I would stop often and give him a hand. I ended up selling for 25,000.

We had taken over a car dealership and fenced off a large city block. We filled it with cats, skidders, excavators and whatever.

44: MY FAMILY WAS KIDNAPPED ? in 1984

One day just before finishing my work near 5:00 and I called my wife Gwen to tell her I would be leaving in a few minutes. She said supper was on the stove and the boys (likely 4-6 ish?) were fine. See you soon. I hung up and the secretary said someone wants to desperately speak to me on line 2. I picked up and they said:

"YOUR WIFE AND KIDS WILL BE KIDNAPPED TOMORROW!"

He hung up. I gasped. Surely not. I was just talking to Gwen.
I called her back **and there was no answer.**
My heart stopped, I nearly fainted.

I called in the secretary and told her to call the police. The special detectives seemed to be in my office before I sat down. They closed down the town, road blocks, everything into full mode... It was very impressive and I was so glad they were there. They sent a number of cars to the house and surrounded it with sirens and lights blazing.

No one was there, GONE...

A moment later a lady with a baby carriage and another on tricycle came up the street. The police asked, "Are you Mrs Priebe?" "Yes" she said. "Please get you and the kids into the police car immediately". Gwen asked "Why ?", " Because there has been a kidnapping threat on you" said the Officer, Gwen laughed.... "Me ??? " and laughed some more. The police escorted her into the car and drove her off with the kids. She asked if they could go to her friend's house and they agreed, but with a police guard.

I got to our friends house and it was now getting late. I said the bank had given me authorization to spend whatever I needed, we can fly away, we can stay at a hotel, whatever.... We thought about it but with all the stress we were coming down with colds and fever. We decided we would just go out for supper and then go and sleep in our own beds, it would be best. After all, the house was and would remain surrounded by police cars and police.

We went out for dinner and the only place open was the old Courtenay House. It was on the seedy side of town and the stripper bar was on the back half. We took our friend along as we thought we at least owned them dinner. Gwen and the kids went inside but I couldn't get the back door of the car to close. It was jammed open. So I went inside and call BCAA. Most interesting call. I was under extreme stress and when I explained to the tow truck guy my problem he thought maybe I was just a drunk who couldn't close his own car door and hung up on me.

I phoned back, please listen I explained, I have two little kids and I really need your help. Where are you he asked. I told him in the back parking lot of the Old Courtenay House. He hung up again. I then noted we were being followed by the police, made sense, so I had them call and the tow truck came and fixed the car.

We could see the two plain clothes guys having coffee next to us, keeping us safe. Our friend kept saying really loud, " MRS. PRIEBE, please pass the ..." She wanted to make sure any kidnappers did not mistake her as Mrs. Priebe.

The next day we stayed home, sick in bed. We talked about flying away somewhere for a few weeks. The bank and police had offered to build us special metal doors with many locks and alarms. We looked at each other and thought, **I don't want to live in fear.** We said no, we are just going to live our lives as they are.

We will trust in God.

The next day was Valentine's Day. Gwen had been eyeing a very expensive warm winter coat at a specialty store but I told her we could not afford it. I got up that morning and bought it for my Valentine. She was much more important to me than the money.

Family first.

45: I once was BLIND, 1982

In the winter of 1982 or so a number of families with young kids went tobogganing on Forbidden Plateau. Likely the Porritts, Larsens, Ryans, Thompsons and Priebes. Never thought of that name "forbidden" until typing this, might have been a sign...

We had a great time on the designated toboggan hill and then after sometime Chris and I were eyeing the old closed ski run behind us. Lets do it. So we dragged the toboggan to the top and with a big shout, were off. What an awesome run. **Fresh untouched deep powder was spraying all around us** and we were flying down the hill in my old aluminium toboggan.

We started to drift to the right but I was not concerned as it all looked very open. Then I saw it, about a 3 feet deep drainage ditch all covered in snow but it was going across our path and there was no time to do anything to avoid it at our speed. Luckily, when they dug the ditch they put the dug up excess dirt on our side which was now all covered in snow but made a good ramp for us. We hit the embankment and it looked a **scene from the Dukes of Hazzard** as we hit the excess dirt embankment at full speed and flew thru the air clearing the ditch by a mile... I can still see it all in slow motion in my head. We landed in the fresh powder and kept going until we reached the bottom of the hill and the crowd of enthusiastic friends cheered our great spectacular flight.

When we had landed I had hit my tail bone on my butt very hard. I got up and Russ came over to give me a big pat on the back for the awesome run. At that time everything was going dark for me. As Russ patted my back I grabbed his arm and said, **" I am going blind, everything is going dark "** Within in a few seconds I was almost totally blind with everything was just very dark shadows and all blended together in a fog of black. Russ said he would guide me to the chalet/restaurant and we would sit down, rest, have a hot drink and he would call the medics. I am not sure of the time frame but it seemed forever, then the light started to return and I slowly regained my sight.

"Once I was blind, but now I see." That line from the song Amazing Grace took on so much more meaning to me after that.

46: BOMB UNDER MY TRUCK ? in 1984

I had been the special debt officer for a few years now and it was really getting to me. I spent most of my days in court or hearings. I remember I settled one court case at a urinal. The lawyers would not let me talk to my previous clients who very honest loggers. I saw one of them head for toilet so I did too. I looked at my old buddy and just said let's settle. He did, we both won, lawyers lost.

I remember one day the bailiff, the lawyer and I walked into a restaurant. The owner saw us and turned white in fear. I said: "No no, we are just here for lunch." Darn it, if he didn't clean the restaurant out and disappear that weekend.

The lawyer and bailiff teased me over our documents as we had put into the contract that we got everything if he failed. I even wrote in the parakeet bird into the document. The bailiff phoned me up one day and said they had found some of the stuff, even the bird, and he had recovered it. He invited me out to celebrate and the lawyer brought in a silver platter with the big silver dome, when he opened it, he said: "Here is your bird". Everyone laughed, it was just a chicken. Every now and then you need a good laugh when you seem to only live on the dark side.

I had taken to drinking hard liquor at the time.

One day I went to get in my truck and as I had been doing this for sometime, I first looked all around for any tampering and underneath for a bomb. I would open the window of the old red van and stood outside the vehicle while I turned it on.

With the car running I sat there while it warmed up thinking, I have to get another job.

I cannot live like this Lord, please help.

47: <u>GOD ANSWERED MY PRAYER , I got Fired. In 1984</u>

My prayer to get out of that job was answered in the most usual backward and unexpected way. I wanted to move on but afraid to take the step, no problem, let GOD give me a little push.

Ok, not so little, I only seem to respond to a total wipeout.

We got the audit at the bank and it became very obvious they needed to lay blame somewhere for our branch having the largest default of loans. Not surprising to me as we had the largest gains in the good times it only made sense we would have the largest default. But someone needed to take the blame and that someone was me.

I was fired.

I took it calmly and just walked out the door with my briefcase.

Times again were very tough and unemployment high, what was I going to do?

The next day I went to Head Office and went straight to the top. I still had access to the whole building. I walked into the head guys office and the secretary greeted me by name. They knew me well.

I said very loudly so that so that the big boss who was just around the corner could hear, as I knew he was listening as soon as she said my name. Likely she said so he would be put on the alert. I said, **"I need one minute of his time or he could talk to my lawyers."**

He came around the corner and welcomed me into his office. I had great respect for him as we had many a great conversation over the years. I simply pulled out a small spreadsheet with the percentage ratio of who had approved what percent of my loan portfolio. I managed it, and yes, was the worst in the province. I deserved to be fired, but as I said, though it was all under my name, I had my limits and most of the loans had been transferred to me from other managers and branches as I was the Special Debt Officer.

I had approved 3% of the loans. The % ratio went up as the name of my manager was above mine, then the names of numerous head office credit dept heads and the largest % ratio of them all, and of Course the largest, were approved by the man I was talking to.

I said, before I give a copy of this to my lawyer, I thought I would show you. I can agree that I deserve to be fired but then all those above me and especially those who approved more % than me should be fired too. After all, that is how business works, doesn't it ?

He passed the paper back to me and told me I was rehired and he would look after everything. I thanked him and went home.

Shortly later I got my wish. My first managership in Greenwood, BC. A town of 800 people in the middle of nowhere. The bank was thinking that Deryl would be out of sight and out of the way, (again) or so they had hoped.

I loved Greenwood.

48: <u>**GREENWOOD! 1984-1986**</u>

We loved Greenwood for the most part and made some life long
friends there too. It is an almost abandoned gold and copper town.
I believe it was the 3rd largest city on the west coast back in 1900.
After World War I copper prices dropped as copper was salvaged
from decommissioned ships and Greenwood became a ghost town
overnight.

Within a few steps from our back door we explored abandoned
mines, and an old smelter. We would cross country ski down the old
railway bed from the top of Phoenix to our back door and hot tub.

I managed two branches, one in Greenwood and the other about 15
minutes south at Midway. On payday we would run the cash needed
back and forth in my car, likely $100,000. ? I had and carried a
pistol which I had never used. I thought it would likely be better to
throw the gun than to shoot as the grip was scotch taped together.

One day as I was doing the drive with a lot of cash on that narrow
and windy road thru the bush and canyon, I turned a corner and there
were two rough looking cowboys. They were leaning against their
car which blocked half the road and each had a rifle held over their
shoulders.

I panicked. I floored it as could not turn around and I made a run
into the other lane and flew around their car ducking below the
dash. As I looked in the rear view mirror I realized that they were
just two local boys heading out hunting.

I called Head Office and told them we were not transporting cash
anymore and they needed to hire an armored car service. Too
expensive they said. "Not nearly expensive as my widow's lawsuit."
I said. We soon had armored car service.

My new boss came into town and wanted me to get more business. I
said good idea, let's talk about how over at the coffee shop across the
street. We walked and when we got half way across the main road
going through downtown, I stopped. He kept talking not realizing
we were in the middle of the road.

I finally stopped him from talking to show him where we were standing for the 5 minutes or more, in the middle of the day, in the middle of the road and not a single car or person in site. I asked, which business do you want me to solicit? We had coffee and that ended any dreams of expansion in the metropolis of Greenwood.

Shortly after, my boss declined a loan renewal application I sent in. He wanted better security. I told him I agreed but I had gone thru this a year before on the last renewal and it ended going all the way to the top and the head guy told me for political reasons to just leave it alone. I said to over turn his decision I would need his approval as he out ranked both of us.

Because I would not do what my new boss said, I was removed from office and demoted to Assistant in Invermere. I know I don't play well and my wife tells me my tone is very rough when I get on my high horse to defend what I think is right. I am not gracious or even considerate or being emphatic. That trait has not served me well. I normally am very understanding and giving to my staff, but intolerant of those in authority, especially when we do not agree.

If you learn anything from my experiences, please learn to consider other people's position and situation. If you still don't agree then be the diplomat finding consensus. Standing up for what you think is right and the attitude of it is either my way or the highway will find you like me, standing at the side of the road without a ride.

Hard on those around you who depend on you too.

49: INVEREMERE 1986-1990

What a gorgeous resort town located on Lake Windermere between the Rocky Mountains and the Cascade Range. We built a house right on the lake.

We got a lot for $30,000 while others like it were $100,000. It was located in Tunnacliffe Flats. I asked why "Flats" when we are 100 ft above the lake on a ridge overlooking everything. After we moved in I changed the name to Tunnacliffe Heights and it became the most prestigious place in town.

A rose by any other name may smell the same, but can sure cost a lot more if marketed right.

It was funny as I was sent there as an Assistant with a demotion but shortly after I arrived the manager got sick and I ran the show for a year or so. My main job was the business loans and I noted the business association had almost died. I walked around and introduced myself to every business and asked: "Do you think we need an association and if so, what would you like to do?" They all said yes, and then told me their passion. I built that association around each of their passions and it became such a success. We turned into a Chamber of Commerce and I was able to unite the four or five communities together into a strong tourist marketing machine.

I had learned from my lesson in Grade 1 to let others pursue their dreams too.

The highlight was the Appreciation Day we created which is celebrated on the closest weekend to my birthday in July. I remember being with the leaders of each resort and community standing side by side flipping pancakes. I had brought them together under a mutual passion of becoming a destination resort area.

I was awarded the Premier of the Province of BC pin for Community Leadership, a great honour.

We attempted to attend a local church as we had not been to church for a few years. Once we got involved in the church the pastor was on my case to raise my hands as he was trying to rally emotional control over the people. He confessed that was his objective.

I said I was just not comfortable doing it, maybe the old Hitler salute or something I don't know, just very uncomfortable for me. I discussed his calling me out during the service, "come on Deryl, you can do it "with him in private. I told him I had no intention on creating trouble or a church split so would keep quiet and just attend.

He had our name immediately removed from the letter slots and asked everyone to "shun us". It was unbelievable, these good people who just a few days before were our friends were now crossing the road to the other side if they saw us coming. In a small town, you cannot help but pump into each other at the store or post office.

We quit church for a season and I focused all my energy into my Community service. A year or two later the pastor left too. The people left never made any attempt to reach out to us. I was good as I had my work and community service but Gwen's confidence was shattered **and she never fully recovered her trust in church people.**

50: OSOYOOS 1990-1992

Next we moved to Osoyoos which is another dream location at the south end of the Okanagan Valley. It is on a lake and considered the only desert in Canada. We got a new supreme leader for the province and he was sales and customer service oriented.

THIS WAS GOING TO BE MY ERA!

I sat down with our new boss and we were of the same mind. I went back and that branch broke every record in the books. We went #1 in most areas and in some cases even across all branches in Canada. I received the Senior Vice President Award for excellence in Leadership, Sales and Community involvement.

I was president of the Chamber, created the Presidents Club to bring the various community clubs like Lions, Kinsmen etc together and even brought in entertainers like Bryan Adams for a concert.

I was nominated for citizen of the year. So I was told.

I HAD ARRIVED and just turned 40 years old.

It was my world and I was in total control.

Church wise we found a good church which was great as the boys were now teens. We had a big games room above our garage where the teens of the church hung out. We had to the dog, Soccer who would go up and chaperon, if anyone every touched anyone else, he would bark until they stopped. Gwen would just shout on the intercom, quit it you two, and all went back to normal.

Note that church just gets an afterthought here, that is where it was in my life too at the time.

51:   AT AGE OF 40, MY CRISIS AND CRASH. In 1991

I heard a loud BOOM !!! and a black cloud of smoke engulfed my son's car. Both my sons were in the car next to me and my heart stopped as I gasped for air. The smoke cleared from the car backfiring and I could see my two sons laughing as they passed their Dad in his big Chrysler with their little Sprint as we climbed the hill just outside of OK Falls.

I didn't not realize it at the time but that was **a tremor before the devastating quake** that was soon to shake my world to its core. **GOD wanted to get my attention.**

We were driving two cars from Osoyoos to Calgary to stay overnight with our friends in Calgary. Lance was on his way to his 1st year at Briercrest Bible College in Saskatchewan or as some call it, Bridal Quest. He had wanted to go Emily Carr School of Arts as he is very talented in his drawing and creating. But, for whatever reason, thank heavens, they were full and he could not go. This was much to his Mom's delight as we were concerned with the drugs and crowd he would be hanging out with there. He had graduated from school and dreaded the thought of staying home all winter with his parents and continuing his job as a clerk at the local grocery store. So we offered to pay his way to Briercrest. We told him he didn't have to study but we knew he would be in good hands there and well feed.

Talking about it being Bridal Quest, when I went to the Youth Rally there in Feb 1969 to see Gwen, whom I married, I also met Gwen's roommate Patricia, who I married in 2012 after Gwen died in 2010. My brother Lloyd went there and met his wife Helen. (i need to check that) Lance ended up meeting his bride Kim there and my other son Chris ended up meeting his wife Cory there too. His took a little longer though. They both attended Briercrest for 3 or 4 years but never met until Chris returned to do a special course there as they were both doing their Masters.

52: BULLYING and DEATH THREAT in 1991

Chris, who was only 16 at the time, was on his way to Prairie Bible School to take his Grade 11 & 12. He was too young to be going away but we had no choice. You see, when we moved to Osoyoos, Chris went to the arcade where the kids hung out. He noticed a group of boys bullying a smaller kids and he stepped in to protect that kid.
What he didn't realize, yet he likely would have anyway, was this gang was the like of the local mafia. They were under age and had no respect for the police or court system. Because Chris stepped in and stopped the bullying of the little kid, their actions turned on him. We tried everything, meeting with the parents, the school and even the police, nothing worked. One day, one of my police friends invited me out for coffee. He told me they had a reputable rumor that my son's life was in danger and he recommended we send him away to a boarding school. This was definitely not a suggestion, so we did.

A few months after we sent Chris away there was a shooting by this gang and someone else died.

Now, some 20 years later, Chris has started his own company called Two Hat Security or Community Sift with the focus on Internet Bullying. He travels the world speaking and promoting this filter to keep children safe. He started by creating what I believe was the world best child filter for Club Penguin back in 2006. At the time it was the world's largest child's internet community game. It is always amazing that when you look behind anyone who has created or done something great, there is usually **a reason for that PASSION.**

Prairie Bible School and College is in Three Hills, Alberta. Chris's grandfather, who became a pastor, as well as many of both my brothers and Gwen's brothers, had gone there and we had numerous friends working there who I had met in my camp days. I mention that as it is always strange how things work. I need to send my son off for Grades 11 & 12 and find out where he is going; two of my very trusted families who also have kids his age and are already there to take him in.

Further, when we arrived and were unpacking his things I heard a voice I recognized in the next room. "Jake" I shouted, sure enough, it was my good friend from when I was in Grades 11 & 12. He was now in the RCMP (Police) and was there as his son was also going to be going to the school too, though they lived close by. Some additional inside protection as he could read the RCMP files and keep an eye on my son.

Funny story how Jake joined the RCMP. In 1968 he and I as teens had spent a night at Playland at the PNE in Vancouver having fun and were driving home. He had a hot car and was way over the speed limit. An RCMP pulled us over. Well Jake could talk himself out of anything as he was a schmoozer and figure he could talk himself out of this ticket. Best way he said was to put the discussion on the other person and take the focus off you. So he schmoozed the Officer.

Jake told him he was interested in joining the RCMP. The RCMP officer told him all about what a great job it was and even took us to his car and showed us the cool stuff and gave him contact numbers. After some time we got out of the RCMP car and were heading back to Jake's car to head home feeling we had pulled it off. The RCMP officer tapped on the window just as were to leave and said, " oh, nice try, but here is your ticket". I laughed, Jake not so much but he had made his career choice.

Seems even the bad experiences in life happen for a reason.

53: <u>VISIT FROM MY FATHER's SPIRIT.</u>

I need to set the stage here a little.
I had just turned 40 and was having the greatest year of my life.
I had won the Senior Vice President's Award at work for having the
most improved and best branch in all of Canada.

I was promoted to Senior Consultant for Western Canada.
I was nominated for Citizen of the Year for all my community work
and leadership.

I had chaired and operated numerous festivals in town as President
of the Chamber of Commerce which included the Cherry Festival,
Santa Claus parade and many more. We also brought in major
concerts to Osoyoos such as Tom Cochran, Righteous Brothers and
even Brain Adams.

To top it all off, I had also been awarded the Premier of BC pin for
Leadership and Community Service, a great honor of which I was
VERY PROUD of and wore everywhere.

Did you count all the "I"'s ? My Scottish born Father-in-law used to
say about me to Gwen, "he is a nice boy, but sometimes the German
really comes out." I was 40, both my boys were heading off to
college, we were empty nesters with the rest of our life in front of us
and I had just been promoted to a very prestigious dream job.

Nothing can stop me now !

We made it safely to Calgary and were staying overnight at our
friends house in Calgary. Gwen and I were sleeping in the basement
and at about 3:00 am I woke up with the feeling someone was
watching me. I looked at the foot of the bed and there was my
Father. He was nodding his head.

This was 1992 and my Father had died in 1988.

Pay attention to that time as many of my spiritual visits happen at
3:00 am, likely because I am too busy during the day.

I never had a real relationship with my Father. Not bad, that was just the way it was and I knew no different. I was the 8th son of 8 boys and my Dad was 43 years older than me. He worked hard to keep the family feed and we normally had another couple or more of my 18 to 20 yr old cousins staying with us too. So Dad was busy with work and dealing with the older boys.

Back to 3:00 am in Calgary, I originally thought that my Dad's visit was to acknowledge the great things I had accomplished and to approve of the way I had raised my sons. But I now realize it was to say, you are not alone, there is a great cloud of witnesses going with you, (Hebrews 12) It was like he was saying "PLEASE SON, PLEASE do not let your sins and pride entangle you **so that you miss out on the great works GOD has prepared for you to do.**

But first, GOD needs to recreate you, to discipline you. You are too proud and believe you can do anything by yourself. You used to fear the correction of your earthly Father but now you are going to experience the correction of your Heavenly Father.

Just know, we will always all be here for you."

Interesting, we saw an excellent live play of SCROOGE last night, this was 2016 when I wrote that part. The years of 1992-1998 seemed to be my Scrooge experience years and the choice as always,

Would I choose to change?

54: I NEVER SAW IT COMING !!!
From euphoria to deepest depression in a second.

We were driving west on a prairie road just outside of Three Hills in Alberta and coming to where the road would go down into a deep valley. I had my eye on the rear view mirror where I could still see my son's school. He was just 16 and we had dropped him off there and were heading home, some 500 miles away. We had said goodbye to our other son the day before in Calgary as he headed out to Saskatchewan for his first year of college.

I was 40 and had just become an empty nester. We had realized that we would become empty nesters at a young age and were REALLY looking forward to the freedom. As detailed in my previous story, we had the world by its tail. Though, a year before we had taken a weekend holiday to Vancouver without the boys and had loaded the car up with chips, pop, jelly beans and any other junk food we could find as we did not have the boys and therefore we did not have to eat "good". We got so sick.

Careful how you use or abuse your freedom.

I lost sight of my son's school in my rear view mirror as the roadway crested the hill and we started down into the valley. From the highest high of now starting our new awesome life to the lowest low I broke into a devastating depression the instant I lost sight of my son's school in the rear view mirror.

I wailed and burst into tears and my heart died. I went into a two year depression that would see me lose my job, my confidence, myself ...

... but I would find my GOD.

55: CONSULTANT or INSULTANT? In 1992-1994

In 1992 things were awesome. I got a big promotion to Senior Consultant for Western Canada. Most of my job was to travel all over BC and help branches to move into the sales world of financial planning. This included going to each branch, assessing how to improve their productivity, rearrange the office both physically and staff wise to accommodate the new sales era.

I soon realized my authority, or more appropriate my recommendations, carried a lot of weight. So much, they were normally fully implemented. This impacted many lives and families. All in all, I laid off 33 people, most of them older managers who I offered enhanced retirement packages. Many of my old colleges did not want it. I usually took them golfing or out for dinner and explained this was not really optional. The package was very good, they would be foolish not to take it.

I was asked to attend an important meeting in the board room in Toronto about the continued transition. Somehow, with all that new power I had I became even more opinionated and arrogant about my ideas as what would work best. The meeting was going well until some guy made a statement that was the absolute opposite of what I thought should happen. I interrupted and stated my point. He countered. I stood up and very emphatically stated my position as the only position!!

As I recall, two guards arrived and escorted me from the room. The gentleman I was disputing was the #2 guy in the bank. I was relieved of my duties and asked to just go home and wait for a reply.

Oh Deryl, when will you learn?

It is not that my idea was wrong, it is the way I say it, my attitude and inconsiderate demeaning tone.

A few days later I was reading the latest statements from the bank and noted that the guy I was arguing with was leaving the bank to pursue other opportunities. Head Office contacted me to come back to Toronto as they liked what I had to say to discuss it further.

I had had it and told them what to do with their meeting. Ok, not in those words but the underlying intent was there. Not the brightest move.

I believe I could have had a very good career in the bank had I learned to play nice. I likely could have pursued them to go with ideas as they did eventually go that way anyway. But my pride and arrogance lead to me to resigning.

That only lasted a few days and I was offered a new dream job. The bank was very patient with me, much more than I was of them.

I got the opportunity to go back and rebuild my old branch in Courtenay/Comox where I got fired from 10 years before.

I got to go "home."

Time wise there is a big story that should go here. How I was stranded for one week and took that time to find GOD and to really start our relationship. I go into detail on that in a later story.

I think some of the best GOD stories come from my two years doing ministry with the Cumberland Boys Club from 1994-1996 which you read in the beginning of this book. **CUMBERLAND,** located next to Courtenay with both being in the Comox Valley on Vancouver Island.

I was told if you can comfortably add "you idiot" to the end of your sentence, you said it wrong.

56: I TRAVELLED TO ETERNITY, and yes, back again. 1996

I had mentioned that my sons and I try to put our pack backs on and disappear into the wilderness once a year. For awhile, we took turns choosing the hike. Whose ever turn it was would organize all the info and then give it as present at Christmas to the other two. One year, Lance organized the West Coast Trail. I opened the present and looked at it with some hesitation, he commented, "Dad, put up or shut up, you have been talking about doing it all your life, let's just do it." We did.

We did it with our good friends Stan Porritt and his three sons hiked the West Coast Trail back in 1996. My other son Chris was in Russia at the time, story to follow.

It took us seven days to hike the 75 km Lifesaving Trail on the rugged west coast of Vancouver Island. People ask me what it was like and I tell them if they have ever wanted to go to military grunt camp for 7 days, go for it.

It is considered one of the hardest trails in the world.

Halfway along we were making good time so decided to just stay at the one campsite all day. Lance and I were sitting on a large rock overlooking the ocean with the waves pounding and breaking on the rock below and the sun giving us a touch of warmth.

I was thinking of nothing at all and then it was like I was free of this earth, free of time. I briefly grasped the concept of eternity. The concept that the universe was unending, that time was no more, that GOD was eternal, always was, always is and always will be and that my Spirit was with HIS now and forevermore.

As quickly as it came it was gone but the feeling of that moment lives on. I am at a point in this vast spiritual journey where I realize that I am the Spirit living in this physical body. One day,

I will shed this body and move on my adventure that will last for eternity.

The GREAT ADVENTURE

to RUSSIA.

In 1998

57: RUSSIA, Fund raise $32,500 in 75 days or no go.

My younger son Chris decided he was going to take a year off his college studies and go to Russia to teach with a group called The Commission. They were invited into the schools in Russia to teach English. After 70 years of Communism, the Western style was not known well by Russians. They would teach western morals and ethics from the concept of Christian principals.

The cost for each person was $32,500. We were not receptive to him going to Russia but would not stand in his way if it was GOD's will. So we said:

1) You need to raise the funds.
2) You cannot start fund raising until you have graduated this year. Not to take away from studies.

He graduated at the end of April and then visited all the churches we had attended to speak and raise funds. Good thing we had attended many churches in various towns. He had to have the funds by July 15th which was the fly date. He left for training in Chicago and had still not received all the monies. On the morning of July 15th, I went to the mailbox to check for cheques, and it was full. I went home and opened all the envelops and added up the cheques, it was just a few dollars over $32,500. Wow. Go with our blessing Son.

Chris flew out of Chicago to Russia. Actually he was going to a place just north of the Crimea area, to the same place **120 years to the day**, i repeat. **to the day,** that my Great Grandfather had left that area. My Grandfather left because of religious persecution and my son was returning to share the gospel.

58: RUSSIA clearing customs with 2 suitcases of BIBLEs

I went to visit him the following spring at Easter. I had asked what he wanted me to bring and he said the people really wanted English Bibles. So I put the word out and ended up with two very large suitcases of new and loved Bibles. I ended up taking all my clothes out as I could wear Chris's clothes when I got there and just took a carry on for me with two very large heavy suitcases with nothing in them but Bibles.

My flight from Vancouver was delayed two hours and therefore all my connecting flights were off. Well, **I figured if GOD wanted these Bibles delivered HE had to get me there.** Many hours later, after stays in Toronto then Frankfurt, I arrived in Moscow very late at night on the last flight that night. I was confused at customs and filled out a German declaration, all in German. When I got to the clerk he talked to me in German which I could not understand. I speak English I said not German. I recognized the language as my parents spoke it when they didn't want us to understand. I ended up in the wrong line so had to go back and fill in an English form and had to go back to the end of the longest line. A number of 747's had just landed. My ride with some of Chris's friends from this airport in northern Moscow was cancelled as I was delayed I would need to find my own way to the local airport some 100 miles away in the south of Moscow.

I had told the people organizing Chris`s stay that I was bringing the Bibles and they did not recommend I do that. They reminded me that this was still Russia which had over 70 years of Communism where Bibles were contraband. I had no way to hide them so just left that up to GOD. They said that the customs would likely confiscate them while they reviewed the literature for …. They said it might go into a store house and likely never be seen again. What would happen to me is they would either keep me until my return flight, or let me go as they had the unauthorized material. No telling as Bibles were legal in Russia now but many of those custom agents worked in the old regime.

Chris had said to make sure I got thru the line quickly as they might run out of taxi's. I ended up in the wrong customs line and then got sent back to stand at the end of a very long line. I was finally getting to the front of the line and the other 5 or 6 lines had since finished and the customs agents closed their wickets and came over to my wicket to help close the last booth so they could all go home.

These custom agents were in Russian military or agent uniforms with big guns and looked very serious. The guy in front of me was from the Middle East or something and had a big box. The customs agents were being very thorough and going thru everything. When they opened his box it had a large lamp or maybe an opium pipe thing. Whatever it was it started a very heated argument. If you have ever heard a middle eastern man scream and yell this man was the best. I thought great, let's get the Custom Agents totally upset. Almost every agent in the building came over and argued and shouted at the man in front of me. I really thought someone was just going to shoot him. Why would you argue with a man in uniform in a foreign country you are trying to get access to, who has a big gun???

Good luck with this one GOD I thought. Why did GOD ever put that man in front of me? Why did I start in a German line and was the last person in the building. One of the Custom Guards took a second from the heated argument of which I must add the hand and arm motions equaled the shouting. He looked at me, the last and only person left in the building. His eyes burned right thru me as his anger raged all over his face. He shouted and motioned to me**.. "GO !!!"**.

I grabbed my two heavy cases of Bibles and went as fast as I could for the outside door.

59: RUSSIA lost in the airport

Chris had warned me about the Moscow taxi drivers but it was 2:00 am and must have had 15 of them trying to grab my suitcases and me. I said the name of the south airport in my best Russian and a man said, YES, and threw my luggage and me into his cab. We drove on the Moscow expressway for many hours in his broken down Lata. I had no idea if he was taking me where I wanted to go. I just said, **"GOD I am going with the Bible's, so if you want them delivered, you gotta get me there."** I must say, **I have never had such peace** and if you talk to my friends who have flown with me other times, I am not a calm traveler. I am more often like that other man in the airport. Friends still joke about my extreme action on other flights.

$100 US later, I arrived at the airport. What an old building. I wondered in history whom had all gone thru this likely before an old beautiful stone train station. From conquerors, Jews and possibly even my Grandparents. There were no flights out till morning and all booths were not only closed, but had big metal garage doors closed. I spent the night lying on top of my bags of Bibles to protect them and people watching.

I saw an old Orthodox Priest wearing black robes and a big cross on a chain necklace with a full white beard. I also saw a large group of Gypsies who had taken shelter in the older part of the building. I ventured over, sat down with my suitcase and watched. They played music and danced, just like you would imagine a Gypsy Colony would spend the night. A Security Guard in full military uniform with a big gun came over to me and asked me to leave that area. He spoke little English, but I gathered that if I stayed, I would be lucky if I woke up in the morning and if I did I would have lost all my stuff and even maybe my clothes.

Morning finally came and birds were flying thru the station.

Ok, now where do I go to get my ticket to get to Chris's small town about one thousand miles south. I wandered the whole station which was very large and finally gave up asking and trying. Well Lord, now what… I heard GOD say, **"See that man with the red hat over there, follow him."** Why not, I was not having any success.
I followed him in what was now a very crowded station. I was glad he was tall and had the red baseball cap or I would have lost him. After many turns and many different rooms and stairs he stopped and got in line. I managed to get in line behind him and asked, "do you speak English". "Yes". "Can you tell me where I would get a ticket to go to Krasnodar?" "You found the right line," he said, "stay with me, I am going there too." After we got our tickets we walked for what seemed miles, up and down stairs and building to building. We got the flight and when we arrived, Chris was waiting for me.

Thank GOD, I was so exhausted,

but at peace.

60: RUSSIAN LIFE a 1,000 miles away from Moscow

Chris lived in the outskirts of Adegha, a town of about 100,000 people but seemed like the village from Fiddler on the Roof. A block away was the farmland where the Russian farmers wore baggy pants tied with a rope belt carrying a homemade hoe and pulled carts with oxen or cattle. You would see Gypsies in wagons heading to town.

The first morning Chris told me we needed milk. I looked in his fridge or icebox and we had none and I told him I did not see any 7-11 convenient stores on our taxi-ride in. He gave me an old milk bottle and a coin and told me to go to corner where the big tree was. There I would find an elderly lady with a World War I water tank hauled by her cow.

I found her and waited in the Russian line under the shade of the big old tree. When I got to the front I gave her my coin and the bottle and she opened the old spigot and poured out one bottle of milk. I took it home very proud of my accomplishment and Chris said, we can't drink that, we need to pasteurize it. So he got out a big ladle and we slowly boiled the milk until we could skim all the fat off the top. "Where did you learn all this" I asked? Then we waited for the milk to cool and had our cheerio's or porridge. That was the Russian way in this village a thousand miles away.

We headed out as he agreed to meet with some of his college friends to give them their English Bible that I had brought. One young lady met us at the bus depot as she was on her to or from work. We handed her the Bible and tears streamed down her face as she gave me a big hug and thanked me and then embraced the book to her chest. She opened the Bible immediately and started to read. Chris said that was normal as they were so used to expecting someone of authority to come along any second and confiscate it in the old days that she just wanted to get at least something read. I think of how many Bible's I have on my bookshelves at home, collecting dust.

We then wandered toward the park to see some statues, the river, dam and waterfalls. We were then going to take the long stairway up to the lookout and have dinner up there. As we walked, college students would see us and join us as they knew Chris.

We stood out big time. Chris had told me not to try and look Russian so that we would not stand out, we would stand out as Western no matter what we did to disguise it. A crowd of college students had now joined us, likely 15-20 and were asking Chris a multitude of questions about GOD. It was like walking with Christ in Galilee and crowds just gathered.

We reached a statue of someone and I asked who it was. All of sudden the college students went into a noisy tyrate telling who he was and how he had saved them from the rape and bilge of the tyranny of the Mongols. They expressed so much hatred and anger and vowed vengeance on the Mongols. Curious I asked, wasn't that like hundreds of years ago? Yes they said and we shall not forget or forgive. One day we will get even with them. This guy was like 20 years old and an educated college student and he **had so much hatred** for something that happened hundreds of year ago. I mean the Mongols from Mongolia are hardly a threat anymore, a couple of goat herders in the high plains of Mongolia? Get over it.

Likely the most heart breaking thing I saw was a young man operating an outside booth selling t'shirts. The one he had was **" I don't deserve to dream". I cried for him.**

We continued on to the restaurant where I figured I was going to have to feed the five thousand but they petered off along the way until there was only a dozen or so. The meal of borsch cost me minimal so I figured that was OK.

61: TWO FATHERS

Another visit was to one of Chris' friends father's house for dinner. His Dad was likely 70 or older and told me stories. He had been in an important high level position in Moscow when Khrushchev took power and was part of the KGB during the Cuban missile crises. I asked him what it was like from their side, as it was sure scary on the Western Side of the Cuban missile standoff. He was a big burly proud KGB type man but that question brought tears to his eyes as he said with his voice cracking in very broken English. "It was that close, it was that close". He said with tears now streaming down his face. He was just a man with his family, not the enemy I grew up with. He asked me how much it cost me to come over. I said about $3,000. He could not comprehend spending such amount or even having such an amount. I dared not tell him how much I made.

Chris lived in housing like a large apartment. Chris`s door to his apartment was a big steel door. Though it is was not sufficient when some burglars came calling one night.

As I recall, what had happened was Chris's room was broken into and things, like his computer were stolen. He reported it and at 2:00 am at night, the police came to interview him. A little history is needed here so you can get the full impact of this meeting.

This was 1996/1997 and numerous states of the old USSR had just broken away from Russia. Some quietly, some not so quietly. Chris was in the Republic of Adega, which is 1000 miles south of Russia, just east of the Crimea and the Black Sea. Some 90 miles from Cehecnea. At this time a major war was going on between Russia and Cehecnea. The Republic of Adega declared their indepenance while Chris was there and declared themselves, (more of less) as a Mulsim country and wanted all westerns out.

Back to the interview, it became apparent to my understading they were not there so much to investigate the burglary, but to find a way to get this Western out of their new country. Chris showed them his Canadian passport and Russian working Visa. They confiscated them as fraud, as they would not recognize a Russian Visa in the new Republic.

Keep in mind, Chris is about 19 years old at this time, on the other side of world, both geographically and socially. He is in a breakaway state from the USSR and teaching Christian morals and Ethics in the schools in predominately Muslim area. GOD help us all, literally.

Communication was difficult at best. Chris would phone home every week or two. It could take 10-15 calls and we were advised to be very cautious at what we said as the calls were likely being recorded. No talk was allowed of a Christian nature. You can imagine our concern as parents when we got the call that our son was being held by the authorities and he needed to go before the judge of this newly broken away state.

I believe they were trying to make a case with Russia and this young Westerner was the ideal platform for their international staging. To make things worse they had gone over as a team of four but their adult leader had found it necessary to get involved in details I still do not feel comfortable discussing. I will say, he was doing 'the Lords" work, for extremely desperate people, but because of it and the possibility of jeopardizing hundreds of groups that had been sent to Russia by the Co-Mission, he was brought home. My son was left there with two other girls his age to complete the mission. Then all this broke out.

At home we roistered as many churches to pray as possible and when Chris had to go before the judge or the political leader, the local school teachers came to his defense saying what good he was doing in the schools. He was given his passports and working visa's back and no more was heard of it, though in Russia, I must say, even when I was there, you always listened for the footsteps as you walked home at night on the dark streets, or as you lay in your bed and you heard someone coming up the stairs.

Maybe just Western paranoia?

62: MIDNIGHT MASS SUNRISE SERVICE

It was Easter, so we tried to take in as much Russian culture as possible. Chris asked if I wanted to go to a Greek Orthodox Midnight mass/sunrise service. I asked which one as one is at midnight and the other is at sunrise. He said they take their church serious in Russia and it was both.

Sure, it would be great to go to church in one of the old Greek Orthodox churches with the large onion shaped roof and the priests with their robes and crosses. Chris said he had become good friends with one of the priests and they had just finished their rebuilding the church. During the Communist era they had used the building as a cement plant. We wandered down a dirt old street with big old oak trees lined the street with a full moon shining thru the branches. The sides of the street had hundred year old small quaint houses. Chickens ran across the road and the occasional old dog would raise his head from a porch to give a single bark. A perfect picture on a beautiful Easter evening in Russia.

We turned the last corner to enter the church and as we looked around the corner and just in front of us…. **and my heart stopped.** I was going to Easter mass in Russia but between me and the church standing shoulder to shoulder on the street was lined with Russian military, with big guns. We would need to go thru them to get to church. What was I doing in Russia going to church and how many of Christians over the years had been stopped from going to church? We had heard many stories when I was child and was not sure if they were true or just western propaganda.

But this militia was not there to stop the patrons from attending church but to facilitate the crowd control. We had come in on the backside of the church and around the corner were thousands of Christian waiting in line to get a glimpse into the church this Easter. We got in line and slowly worked our way to the entrance doors of the church. The way they had it all pews were taken out and the crowd just shuffled in and in a slow procession was shuffled out the two side doors. While you were in the church you could witness the service.

The big white bearded priests carry the large gold crosses and banners and sprinkling ..... As they walked. It was an awesome service.

We went out the front and then got in line again to go thru the church one more time. I am sure more people were in line to watch this Easter Mass than in line for Splash Mountain at Disneyland. Wow. When the sun rose the priest and all their banners and crosses came outside and marched round the church in a big parade singing glorious songs:

to our GOD, our mutual FATHER.

63: **<u>HEARING IN TONGUES</u>**

On Easter Sunday we attended a number of churches. The first met in a gym, very much like our service back home in Gibson's, except in Russian. Chris's interpreter was translating the service for me and I felt it was interrupting the service. I asked him to stop as it was disrupting the service and I could understand perfectly. He was not a believer and questioned how I could know what they were saying as he knew I could only speak a few words (very poorly I might add) in Russian. I told him what the pastor was speaking on and what the little old ladies testimony was. To my Baptist friends, I am not saying I can speak in tongues but I did hear in tongues that day.

The next service was in a big old Baptist church. We sat in the balcony and it was full. In front was the choir, the pastors, and to the left facing us were the Elders. There were likely 12 men, some were very old. Their faces looked like those dried apple doll faces. I thought, what had these men been thru in their lives. They likely were Christians before the revolution and kept their faith for 70 years of persecution and now they had earned the right to sit in the elder's chairs. Maybe not earned the right, but in my eyes, they did.

I remember we sang **<u>"His eye is on the sparrow"</u>** and it sounds just as beautiful in Russian. It took me back to the week I met GOD at Three Hills when I was struggling with does GOD really care about me?

The last service we attended that Easter weekend was in the old Communist party auditorium. You could still see the shadows on the walls of the hammer and sickles from long ago where the paint was not as faded as that around it. I tried to visualize the meetings and what was said. Was it for good or hatred? We had come to hear an Easter choir sing.

They sang songs of the cross and resurrection in Russian but I knew most. Then I heard the orchestra start on an anthem I know and love dearly, Handel's Messiahs, The Hallelujah Chorus.

Immediately I wondered if these Russians here in the old Communist Party Auditorium would recognize Christ as King of King and Lord of Lords and stand at for the Hallelujah Chorus.

A little old man was sitting beside me. Another one of those dried apple doll face people. He was the first to move as he struggled, braced himself on his cane and raised himself up before the first note was sung. He then removed his hat, put down his cane and with tears streaming down his and my face, as we stood there together, this Russian and me, listening to this wonderful chorus our mutual King and Savior, Jesus Christ our Lord.

64. Russian on Salvation

I talked to one of Chris's Russian college students he was mentoring and they were very interested in becoming a Christian and studying the Christian life. Curious, I asked, "what would you need to actually become a Christian." She said,"I think I will look at it for 20 years or so and then make up my mind."

I was blown away. What a different this concept was from our Western culture of "Be Saved today"! I have contemplated that answer all these years, a different culture. Not our fast food, fast service, fast everything and want it now culture and then just throw it away.

Easy come, easy go.

65: RUSSIA: TO THE MOUTAINS

One day Chris asked if I wanted to go to a rugged mountain park with lots of waterfalls or the resorts (actually it was Sochi, where the winter Olympics were) at the Black Sea. I said let's head for the bush and the waterfalls, no surprise.

We went to the train station but were not allowed into the station and had to board the train in an adjacent cow pasture. Reason was the Independent fighters were targeting the train stations to bomb. I just had to get a look at this old beautiful train station so talked to a soldier and got permission to run in, take a quick look and get out. I was glad we chose the mountains as we found out later that three train stations on route to the Black Sea were bombed.

The train was very old, the tracks had sways and dips. The train had to go very slow as the track could not handle fast. I love trains and this was an awesome experience in the far woods of that country. The inside of the passenger cars were like an old western movie with wooden benches and all..

The first falls were close by and the river a torrent with spring runoff. We were going down a slippery trail and I got separated from Chris for a minute. I slipped and ended up running to the bottom of this gulley to keep my balance thru the trees. When I landed at the bottom of this forest gulley, a Russian man had the same problem coming down the other side and we almost slid and crashed into each other. My heart pounded as I thought how many times as a child in the 1950/60's did I play in the bushes as a spy in enemy territory. The enemy was Russia at the time during the cold war.

Now I stood face to face with this very Russian looking man, and me, a very western looking man in an isolated forest ravine in Russia. Directly his small children came down his trail to join him and Chris came down from my side. Two fathers out with their children on a Saturday hike. How things had changed and what it would have been had we meet like this in 1962. We ventured to the lookout and the man followed us. He could speak a little English and Chris some Russian. With it we had a great talk.

Next we headed up the river to the other falls. We had to go past one place where we were about 100 feet directly above the river. With the runoff the river had worn away the trail and we needed to hold onto a rope. We scaled the slope with a raging white water river (like Hells Gate in the Fraser River) was below us. I got across and carried on and then realized Chris was not behind me. I ran back and he had let go of the rope and was sliding down the slippery slope. I grabbed the rope and managed to get his hand and bring him back up to safety. I still have nightmares today of him sliding down that slope and ending in that torrent just above the gorge and falls. **Thank you GOD.**

The trip home was good. I had a full day to be in Moscow which is a beautiful city. I hopped on the subway to go the Kremlin and other tourist points. The subways are very deep with very longgggggg stairs or escalators. Beautiful art work on the walls but reading the names in Russian stations was difficult for me. So many letters looked the same. I got lost and got tired of trying to find someone who spoke English so I sat on a bench and sang 'I'm a poor little lamb that has lost his way". I figured the only people that would understand would be able to speak English and sure enough, soon enough they showed me where I was on the map and which way to go. Hard to tell when you are hundreds of feet underground and the subways do not go in straight lines. Too much like real life when we lose our way, we need help to get home.

Russia is a beautiful and very diverse country and I look forward to seeing much of it more another time. (Careful what you wish for)

What an experience, what an adventure.

66:   28 years CAREER OVER up in smoke. In 1998

I loved my time at the bank for the most part but no job is perfect.

Most times people said I bled the company colours as I was so loyal. The problem was, I had a vision that I saw them being but did not always align with what senior management's image of itself was, or at least the path to getting there. This created an ongoing love/hate relationship of which, it not being my company, I never learned to "come onboard".

People often asked me as well, what are you doing working in a bank, you just don't seem to fit that Bank Manager mold. So true.

I think I was fired about 3 times or more and quit about the same.

I think the best part was that we got to see and live all over the beautiful province of BC. I told my kids not to complain about moving so much when people would say, your poor kids, moving every other year. We got to meet great people who have become life long friends, played new golf courses and skied new ski hills. We were involved in local festivals and hiked the Rockies and camped on the beaches of the West Coast as our back yards.

My last year with the Bank I was in Gibsons Landing, just a short ferry ride north of Vancouver. My bosses had one plan for me, GOD had another. I was torn between the two loyalties and ended up making it a major drama ordeal.

Building my career with the bank I always thought I could have made it to the top. The problem was I did not take the time to think it thru and just flew by the seat of my pants and believing that my talents and skills would be sufficient. I only had my Grade 12, and from night school I might add, though that was not an issue, but I should have taken the Bank courses and degrees while in the bank if I wanted to get ahead. But likely the worst part was I did not make friends in the higher places. I continually challenged those above me to the point that they feared me.

I will still say I was right, but the way I went about proving it was totally wrong and did not and will likely never work. That is bull headed by pushing your own agenda and in many cases, bullying.

In a lot of ways, I did very well. I won the top awards in the Bank across Canada many times for #1 in sales, staff and team building, community leadership etc and each time I would get a big promotion, flaunt my ideas further to people above me who either saw me a threat to their advancement or threat to their job.

Either way, I did not use good people skills to ever try and cooperate or befriend them, they were in my way and needed to change or get out of my way. Life does not work that way.

I needed to respect and maybe even love others on their journey.

67: DAWSON CREEK in 1998

A good friend of mine once said, **"Deryl, you don't burn your bridges, you nuke them!"** Regretfully, he was right. Eventually, when you nuke or burn enough bridges, there is no more escape. You are alone and have to **face yourself.**

Face that, I was the problem.

This was the last chance I had with my almost 30 year career at the bank. My entire career I had stood up for what I thought was right, no matter whom it hurt, and I hurt many. To them I apologize. A Senior Official told me that no one in bank would hire me, I was a loose cannon, a threat to any manager that I might turn on them and destroy them. Fantastic potential but deadly poisonous.

I had one friend left in authority and he was in charge of the North and a job opened in Dawson Creek. GOD and I talked about it and HE wanted me to apply. HE had a different purpose in mind though.

I had told myself back in 1979 when I left Prince George that I would never go any further north again beyond the TransCanada Hyw. The winters were just too cold and too long. But finally I agreed to go. This was 1998.

Then GOD reminded me of when I was 16 and broke my promise to HIM and my Mom at the Ft St John camp. I promised that I would not do anything foolish and that I would not swim across the river. I did though, it was a direct act of rebellion, no other reason. I had witnessed and actually been the person that cried out to GOD to save Cal and HE did, immediately, just moments from his death.   The awesomeness of GOD and the miracle was just too much for me and swimming across that river was my way of trying to take "normal" back.   Take control back.

I agreed that I would return to that river and repent. GOD said that was sufficient as my heart had shown what HE wanted and my actions would not be needed. Do not go to Dawson Creek HE said, your family needs you down here, move closer to your family.

At the time, my eldest son was in Kelowna and my youngest in Russia, but he was coming home soon. *We all live in Kelowna now and that is the biggest blessing of them all.*

My son once told me to stop moving where I can have a job and move to where I want to be and then look for work there. So I did, and we moved to Kamloops.

After all the problems I had been thru in Gibson's, losing my ministry and my job. When I surrendered and even agreed to go all the way to Ft St John just to correct a wrong, all things turned good. I got a job as manager of a Canada Trust office in Kamloops and our house that had been listed for months and no lookers, got a looker that day. They only stayed in the house less than a few minutes so figured no way, but shortly after got a call and sold for full price.

Most people didn't like our house as it was very out of the way. These people did, as we found out later, they turned it into a grow op. (grow marijuana). GOD uses all kinds of people.

It was time to move on.

68: MEETING HARRY, again after 40 years. In 1999

I had moved to Kamloops and Gwen was to follow once the Gibson house sale went thru and we had access to our Kamloops house. I decided to hit some golf balls. I was going to go to Rivershore Golf Course where we had a corporate membership but decided not to go there and turned around after almost getting there. Then I decided to go to McArthur Island but ended up pulling into another one as I was driving past Mount Paul. All the driving range pads were full except for one. I started driving balls. (do you see the set up yet ?). The guy beside me said, "Nice shot", I complimented him. I could see he was there with his son who was about 10 yrs old and he was spending some time with him showing him how to golf.

I was done so got in my car and headed out. I drove to the road and then turned around as I just had to say something to that man on the pad beside me. I went back and said to him, "It is really great to see you out there with your son." I told him to treasure the moments as before he knows it his son will be grown and out on his own. Both of mine had been gone for about 7 years now.

He thanked me and said," It seems I should know you." I agreed. We went thru places we had lived and what we did but could not come up with anything the same. Then we got the brilliant idea of asking, so what is your name. Harry Bicknell he said. Your kidding, not Harry Bicknell who grew up as a kid in Surrey? Yes. Well, we had gone to the same church when we were teens and more importantly played golf together with my nephews Blake and Ross. We used to play 6am to 10pm in the summer at **Hazelmere Golf Course.**

"So what are you doing?" I asked, Harry said he was the pastor at Summit Drive Baptist Church. Really, we just bought a house down the street. I said I have to stop by some Sunday.

Then I started to tell him my son had just got back from Russia and was the pastor at a little church in Nordegg. That he had just finished there and would be coming home for the Labour Day weekend for a visit as he was planning on going to Madagascar as a missionary. We'd come to his church on that weekend.

Labour Day Sunday, Gwen, Chris and I went to church at Summit Drive. Harry was greeting people at the door so I introduced my family. With that he took Chris by the arm and said he would like to buy him lunch tomorrow to discuss being his Youth Pastor. Apparently his previous Young Pastor had just resigned on Friday. (great timing) Chris was not receptive but his Mom talked him into at least going to the luncheon and hear what he had to say.

Chris took the job and we got to spend another four years with our son at home, as an adult. He had basically been gone for seven year. I am so grateful for that time and Chris was awesome in helping the church in their growth over that time and he also got some critical training. We learned later that a missionary that went to Madagascar was killed.

Now, some 12 years later (wrote this section in 2011) and in-numberable wonderful golf games and amazing times at Summit Drive Church, Harry is going to marry me. Ops, I better reword that, Harry is going to officiate at the Wedding between Patricia and I. When Patricia called me and asked if it would be OK if we had the wedding reception at the Hazelmere Golf Course, I thought I'd died and gone to heaven. Wow, how perfect. Harry and I are going to bring our clubs along and will hit at least one drive for old time's sake.

So glad I went back to encourage that man at the driving range.

Soooo many good things or is that GOD things, came out of it.

NOTE: in 1999
Most of these stories are in chronological order. This is where the first story in this book about Chris and I climbing the mountain and GOD parting the cloud along with the next story of us in the cave should be. Somewhere between me meeting Harry again and Chris taking the job with him.

69: Mount Robson, THUNDERSNOW , in 2000

My son Chris and I put the backpacks on as we try to do every year
and headed out to hike around Mt Robson, the highest mountain in
BC. Gorgeous hike thru the valley of a thousand waterfalls and
camping at Berg Lake. The lake is named as full of calved icebergs
from the towering Mount Robson's glacier which flows from near
the top down into the lake.

The next morning we wandered out a short distance to a glacier and
into an ice cave. What colours and crystal, beautiful. We then
ventured a little further as wanted to just see over the next ridge, then
the next pass and across to the pass on a scary rope bridges and a
very narrow steep trail looking down a thousand feet to glaciers
below and towering peaks above.

We turned around at about 2:00 pm as it appeared a storm was
coming and we had likely wandered too far. We had not brought
proper clothes or provisions as only thought we would venture a
short distance but now we were miles from camp. We picked up our
pace as we had a few miles of rugged mountain trails that were not
too well marked. As the snow started we realized the trails would be
lost once the snow covered the ground. The last mile we were
running. The snowflakes were gorgeous, very large and nearly a
white out. We were down in the alpine trees and just made it to
camp to see our tent had collapsed under the weight of the snow.
We moved into a cabin they had built for emergencies and this was
one.

We heard a loud roll of thunder which echoed thru the valleys then
the largest flakes I have ever seen fell in what they call
thundersnow. I just had to thank GOD that my son and I were
standing on the covered deck of the cabin witnessing this winter
wonderland of snow falling so hard it was a total whiteout and that
we were still not out on the mountain trail.

**Our journey in life is like that. We need to venture out if we
want to see the wonders of GOD, but also need to stay alert, be
prepared and watch for the warning signs to know when to run
for Shelter.**

70: WOULD YOU FOGIVE A PEDOPHILE ? in 2002

I believe one of the most important things to living life is to FORGIVE.

So many relationships have been lost because of the inability for people to forgive. I have seen so many groups and even churches that have been torn apart as one party cannot forgive another.

To truly forgive. Do you? Can you?

Would you forgive a Pedophile? Not likely, and if you are like I was, you would cheer over their death. I have known a number of pedophiles in my life and talked about a few in my stories, like at camp.

In about 2001 I took a group of men from our church to a Promise Keepers weekend at 108 Mile House. Promise Keepers at the time was working on the "Purity Series" which mainly deals with the issue of pornography. Promise Keepers in the book "Every Man's battle" used to joke that 95% of men have a problem with pornography and the other 5% were lying. ha ha.. But latest surveys show that a large majority of men are battling or have battled with it. Also it has been shown that the stricter a man is brought up the higher the percentage, as it is a secret "sin".

Back to the weekend. Friday night was awesome. A little old church up at 108 mile house was packed with men singing and praising GOD. The speaker hit home on how when GOD made Man and Women HE made them in HIS image. Not individually, but together they are in the image of GOD. He also went into how Satan's greatest weapon to destroy man, GOD's greatest creation, is thru sex outside of marriage and Satan's best tool is pornography.

It starts almost harmless, just curiosity, kind of like I did at age 5, but then like any addiction, you need more and more. They say it is stronger than heroin. It ends up consuming the individual and destroying lives and families.

We had a big bonfire afterwards and many guys drove home and back with their junk and burned it.

Saturday we went into "Being the Man God made you to be" type stuff and then Saturday night he got into forgiveness.

- How many of you want forgiveness for what you have done wrong? Put up your hand. I think every hand went up.

- How many cannot forgive yourself for what you have done ? Put up your hand. Again, almost every hand went up.

- How many of you were abused by a pedophile ? Sounded like most hands went up as most had their heads down.

- How many of you feel you are beyond any forgiveness ?

There was a big rugged old wooden cross at the front and almost every guy went up to write down what they were sorry for, what they had done wrong, what they wanted to be forgiven of and used a nail and nailed that paper to the cross. To be forever forgiven, forgotten and forgave. There was not a dry eye in the place as all the men gather beneath the cross together.

****
After everyone was seated again, he asked us all to bow our heads and they turned the lights almost off.

- How many of you are a pedophile ?

I have never heard such silence as we turned from focus on the Abused to the Abuser. Everyone bowed further down and just wanted to crawl under their pews and hide. Likely about six guys as I recall confessed to being pedophiles and he asked them if they wanted to come up to the front, by the cross, nail their sin to the cross and ask for forgiveness. They went forward but could not write their sins down or nail them to the cross. They felt then did not deserve forgiveness nor did they believe anyone or even GOD would ever forgive them.

Then he asked this, " would any of you who are still in your seats like to come up, lay hands on these men and pray for them:

 - Be the representative of the child abused and offer them the forgiveness.

- Pray with them to GOD for their forgiveness.

- Would any of you who have been abused want to come up and have these men represent your abuser and forgive them.

Likely the hardest thing I have ever done, but I got up in the dark, approached one of the men and we hugged, cried and prayed in each other's arms at the foot of the cross.

There was a healthy, holy cleansing that took place that I could never describe. Not only had I forgiven, but in the same way, I was released of my anger, my hatred and the frustration within me.

I was finally free.

71: THE POWER OF HATRED

You might ask what does that anger and hatred look like. Let me tell you.

In 1992 I lived in Osoyoos. At that time if anyone talked about a pedophile or if it came up on the news, I would leave the room. That word brought such anger up in me that I could not contain myself to speak. I know many, when I tell this story at this point I would say **the only good pedophile is a dead pedophile.**

One night, I pulled into the Shell Gas station on the west side of town to fill up. I got out and noticed that one of the pedophiles I knew was filling his tank up in the bay next to me. I opened my trunk and took out my baseball bat and went over to him and crushed his skull. As he dropped to ground in a puddle of blood I continued to hammer him with the bat until all my anger was vented.

I slowly made my way back to my car and put the bat in the trunk and drove away. No guilt, only relief.

I woke up the next morning expecting the police to come to my door. After all, I was well know in town as I was the President of the Chamber and local Bank Manager. The gas station owner who witnessed it all from his window was a client of mine. No police.

I checked the bat in my trunk and it was there but there was no blood on it.

I drove to the gas station on my way to work. There was no blood, no police tape. I went inside and saw the owner. I asked him if there had been anything exciting going on around there last night? Nope.

I drove to the police station just a few blocks away and stopped in to have coffee with the boys. I did that as I had a number of friends in the force. We chatted, I asked if anything exciting had happened last night and they said, nope, quiet night last night.

So I guess I was dreaming, or had had like a Christmas Carole Scrooge type visit. Either way, **I realized that the anger inside me was so great, that I could actually commit murder**. I really needed to do something about it. I had to learn how to forgive so I could move on with my life. **My hatred was destroying my life.**

In the Lord's prayer in the Bible from Matthew 6, it says:
"'Our Father in heaven,
hallowed be your name,
your kingdom come,
your will be done,
on earth as it is in heaven.
Give us today our daily bread.
**And forgive us our debts,
as we also have forgiven our debtors.**

And lead us not into temptation,
but deliver us from the evil one.

Strange, did you notice, GOD does not say "Help me to forgive others as You have forgiven me" but for GOD to "forgive me as I have forgiven other." OUCH.... but then Jesus emphasis this with the next verse:

For if you forgive other people when they sin against you, your heavenly Father will also forgive you. But if you do not forgive others their sins, your Father will not forgive your sins.

Forgiveness is critical. I had to forgive, before I could deal with my anger, frustration and hatred which was destroying my life and finally be free and live in love and peace.

72: DOWNSIZED AGAIN,
what does GOD have in mind NEXT in 2002

I started with Canada Trust in Kamloops and shortly after starting, the TD bank bought them out. They utilized my skills that I had from previous years of doing the dirty work of merging branches. I believe Kamloops had 3 Canada Trust offices and I think 3 TD branches and all that was needed I think was likely 3 in total.

After we finished merging the branches, I got a call from my boss to meet me for coffee at the local hotel. Oh…. I know that game from my years of being the "Exterminator", as I had laid off some 33 people, mostly managers. I packed up my boxes and went home for lunch. I told my wife I thought I was going to be laid off that afternoon and she was shocked. **I said, "no worries, I am just curious what GOD has in store for us next."** Such a difference from the drama of only a few years before when I got my downsizing exit package from the other bank.

Sure enough, I got to the hotel he had said to meet for coffee and there were the lawyers, councillors and my boss. Blah Blah Blah, we have too many managers between the merged TD bank and Canada Trust and needed to downsize. I was reminded I was neither historically TD green or Canada Trust red, I was from the other banks colours, so was being let go. They slid the envelope across the desk. I said a few words that could have been mistaken as a legal action and slid it back asking them to double it and I would leave with no trouble. They doubled the amount and we parted.

For some crazy reason, I had a big smile on my face. I was free. Unemployed sure, but free to do what I wanted, what GOD wanted.

Amazing thing is that, the day before I saw my neighbor down the street was blasting out a ton of rock to build a new house. I said, rather than trucking that rock miles away, why you don't just drop it on my back yard as the road went right past it just a few houses away.

I wanted to build a large terraced rock retaining wall as it was about at 50 foot steep sloping lot and wanted to plant trees and shrubs. He agreed and when I came for lunch that day he had dropped 10 dump truck loads into my back yard. Wow, much more than I expected, but turned out to be the exact amount I needed.

Gwen asked when are you ever going to have the time to do that. The next day I was off for the summer.

After being laid off on July 2, 2002, I decided to take the summer off as I had never had one. Even when I was young I worked for my Dad in the summer. The labour of moving all that rock and dirt by wheelbarrow and building the terraced rock garden was the best thing for me that summer.

73: STARTED MY OWN BUSINESS in 2002

I started my own business that fall and have operated the business for almost 15 years now and love it. Gwen was very nervous and wanted the guaranteed pay cheque. I said I had got the double amount on my buyout so when that ran out, I would get a secure job. We never touched it.

Well almost, one day a number of months into running my own business I came in and was going to quit. I called my good friend to tell him I was going back to the banks. He was not in yet so I left a message to call me ASAP. Before he called me back I got three calls from big prospective clients who wanted to sign up with me. I was flying high when my friend finally called back. I have not looked back since. Thank you Lord.

I would have never left the safety and security of the big corporate banks would I not have been downsized. In hind sight, this is the best thing work related that ever happened. GOD pushed me out of the nest and now I can fly. I just wish I had the faith in my first time I got downsized.

Would have saved me and those around me the unneeded stress.

74: FAREWELL TO SUMMIT DRIVE CHURCH: in Sept 2007

We decided it was time to leave Kamloops and move to Kelowna because that is where the Grandkids lived.

Summit Drive Church under Pastor Harry was where we healed. When we got there in 1999 after a major drama time for the past years and we found rest and rebuilt our faith and confidence. That last Sunday morning service I was to give a little farewell speech. When I got on stage GOD gave me something else to say than what I had planned.

I thanked the Church for all they had done in taking us in and provided that safe harbour for us while we got back on our feet. I quoted a Psalm that was perfect to describe it all.

Then said that we were now ready to go back out to sea, so to speak. A ship is not built to stay in harbour but sail on the sea when sea worthy for the coming storms.

I got off the stage and made my way to the back where I wept bitterly in my friends arms as I realized that a very large storm was coming.

75: IT IS CANCER, NO CURE !!! in Jan 2008

"It's cancer... there is nothing we can do... maybe 5 months to live."
We hung up the phone which was followed by SILENCE.

Everything changed in a moment after the Doctors phone call in
January 2008. We were expecting him to say to my wife Gwen of
almost 40 years, that she had pneumonia, take an antibiotic for a few
weeks and all will be fine, but no, it wasn't. It was mesothelioma an
environmental type lung cancer with no cure and at her stage they
gave her 5 months would be the longest life expectancy.

Gwen decided she would share her story with people rather than to
keep it a secret and to try and help them. **Also, this is what our
faith, our hope is made of and she was going to accept her fate
and leave it in GOD's hands.** Her goal was that when her friends
came to see her that they would not get depressed but would leave
inspired. She did that amazingly well. Not once did I hear her
complain or feel sorry for herself.

I remember one visit to the doctors and reality had not set in yet or
maybe didn't appear it had as we were taking it so well, the doctor
took me aside, looked me in the eye and said, " she will not be here
at Christmas, do you understand that !?"

We are not sure where she got the cancer but the best theory was
from the house they lived in at Clearwater, BC in the 1960's. Her
Dad was a pastor and they lived in the parsonage there which was an
old log house with a wood furnace in a dirt floor basement. You
know, the one where Gwen served me breakfast after we hit the cow
heading to wilderness camp when we were just 16. Clearwater is
marked as one of the highest radium or radon gas places known. In
the winter the old log house would be totally covered in snow,
encapsulated almost and with the dirt floor basement it would have
trapped all the radon gas seeping up thru the ground.

Gwen's Father and Mother died of cancer along with her brother
Bert. All at about age 60. Many times Gwen would tell me she
didn't expect to live beyond her 60th birthday. She died at age 60.
 Careful what you believe and say.

When her Mom died in 1971 and then her Dad, we decided that savings for retirement was not going to be our goal but rather to live our life to the fullest as we go. We made many friends and every year did a major trip.

The only survivor of Gwen's immediate family is her brother Bob. He never lived in the Clearwater house.

Mesothelioma is cancer of the lining in the lung. What I understand is things like asbestos fibers get stuck in the lining of the lungs like little spikes. They rub and irritate the lungs or lining which causes a build up of fluid. The fluid is not in the lungs but between the lungs and lining. As it fills up and there is nowhere to drain the fluid fills that space and compresses the lung. At some point it will suffocate the person and they die.

At first Gwen's lungs would take a month or more to fill and we would go the hospital and have it drained. The problem the doctors said was each time they pierced the lining to drain the lungs it would scab over and that eventually they would not be able to get a tube in. Before that happened they operated and put a permanent tube in which came out of her chest. Now when we needed to drain it I would just attach a vacuum bottle to the tube, open the valves and it would suck all the fluid out. We lived with it but Gwen could not bath which she loved to do for hours. (actually she still did anyway)

We started at having to drain the fluid once a month, then every other week, then every week and then daily. On New Year's Day, Jan 1, 2009 it did not work. We believed the inside end had scabbed over. I phoned the specialist and we all rushed to emergency and straight into the operating room.

I must say, that whole 12 months of doctor and hospital visits that everyone was awesome. They were very helpful, caring and if we needed anything, a scan, surgery, tests, or whatever, it happened and happened now.

I cannot say as much for the cancer clinic. The issue of course was that there was nothing they could do. They offered radiation and we even went on an experimental drug for a few days. My frustration with them was any questions I asked about other types of treatment I had read online, their answer was always..." We don't know anything about that". We decided NOT to return to the cancer clinic as it was very depressing to see others in various stages and they could do nothing for us, there was no good reason to return.

Back to emergency on New Years day. The full specialist staff showed up and tried everything they knew to try and get the tube to drain but we could not drain the fluid. Gwen was drowning and time was now down to minutes. The Lead Doctor, an awesome loving man, took me by the hand and led me out of the operation room. He said, "she only has a minute or so to live" and I walked back into the room to say goodbye.

The Doctors all stood back with a look of total failure, hanging their heads and then .....

SWOOSH !!!! The fluid poured out the tube which now was not attached to any vacuum bottle or machine. The fluid sprayed around the room as the tube looked more like a loose fire hose. When it was finished spraying the tube blew out of Gwen's chest and across the room. Gwen just laid on the operating table, fully awake and unsedatete the whole time, quietly watching. Now her and all our eyes were WIDE as we watched GOD perform HIS miracle.

Gwen lived a total of 30 months from the diagnosis not the 5 months they had stated.

After the New Years Day tube blow out they did not try and put it back in and she lived the remaining 18 months with no tube, no hospital visits and no specialists and she could bath with a full tub. During that time we had hundreds of visitors who came to say goodbye and left inspired. We did about a dozen trips, mainly cruises as they were the easiest and we would take her friends along.

We were worth a few million at the time and I told Gwen;" We have made this money together, let's spend, share or give it away together. I can remake it again if I want when you're gone." It was an amazing blessing and lesson to help so many people to take them on a cruise they could never afford, buy their new car or house. I am free from the slave to work and money. (well, better anyway)

Many friends asked why GOD didn't heal her and why she died so young. I would say, GOD did heal her, twice. First time was in 1972. She was just 21 years old and just after her Mom died of cancer, Gwen was diagnosed too. Then when she went in for her treatment they could not find any cancer, so they told her to go home and enjoy her life. We did. She got another 40 years, had two great sons, got two wonderful daughter-in-laws and she got to play with 5 grandkids as well as the hundreds of lifetime friends she made and blessed.

76.. GWEN's JOURNEY goes beyond THIS LIFE, Her death.

After the New Years day miracle in the story above, the Doctors stitched Gwen up and sent us home. We were waiting for the next fluid buildup of which we had no defense, but it never came. The tubes were out and Gwen could fully bath as she loved and we could travel.

For the next 18 months we had a very good life. **We commented to each other that if we could have learned to live with each other and love each other like this we could have had the best marriage ever.** Our previous almost 40 years were a lot of arguing, correcting and so many mega screaming matches of things I can no longer remember what they were about.

To just forgive, let go, let be and live in love and harmony, no needed to be right, no need to correct or advise.... just care for each other.

We did our last cruise with our friends Heine & Mary and got off the ship June 30, 2010. Gwen was in a wheel chair and would tire very easily and I dont think we got off the boat in the 14 days. Her passport for travel expired that day and she said she did not want to renew it. She just wanted to go home until it was time to move on.

One day we were sorting her things, she liked to that and we found a dime in behind all the clothes in cupboard. Tears ran down her face. "What?" I asked. We sat on the floor and she explained that since she got sick, she had missed her Mom dearly. She had always regretted that she died when she was only 20. Gwen was now 60, because she wanted to talk to her so many times. Then one day when she was feeling sorry for herself, she found this dime in a strange place and it was the year of her Mom's death, 1972. (I think) She took that as a sign either from her Mom or from GOD, does not matter which, but they were there, with her.

"Because if Jesus is always with us and my Mom is with Jesus, she is with me too." She said, "**when I die, if I am able, I will talk to you in dimes.** Don't know if it will be me or most likely be GOD, but know, that when you get a dime, the great cloud of witnesses are with you."

I have since had over 30 amazing dime stories, all at critical times and so appropriate. Those stories are coming up later.

After we got home from the June 30th cruise, Gwen slept most of the time. I would wake her up in the morning to give her the pills and then wake her for lunch and pills, then again for supper. Usually in the evening she would be up for few hours and we would watch her favorite TV shows.

With all this time being a caregiver I had put on about 40 pounds. My brother Glen stopped by and hardly recognized me. He told me I had to do something so I did. I got a golf membership at the little Mission Creek Golf course. I would give Gwen her lunch and put her back to bed then I would go down to the golf course, cell phone on in case she needed me, and walked and played from 1:00 pm to 5:00 pm when I would go home and prepare supper. It was good exercise and good outside therapy for me. I played 85 days in a row and got my handicap down from a 16 to 0. Actually shot an 8 under one day. You will read that story later of my amazing walk with God on the golf course.

Then on Tuesday, Sept 21, 2010, I was playing the 14th hole alone and when I came to make my shot to the green the whole green was covered with crows or ravens, hundreds of them making a lot of noise. I had just walked past that green when I teed off on 13 and I saw none. You might see one or two around but never hundreds. Elijah, the prophet has always been my main man in the Bible. In the story of Elijah, crows or ravens played a major role in his life. I have always found they have been in my life too. When I was wondering if I was going the right way a raven would come and fly with my car for a distance until I knew I was going on the right path, then be gone. A friend was playing hole 13 and shouted out, wow, look at that, never seen the likes. I replied, I believe it is a sign, a sign that my golf is over and I am to go home.

With that my phone rang, first time in the 85 days that Gwen called me. Come home please she said, I want you to call in the family, I am done and want to go home. I want to go and be with my Mother, my Father, Nannie and GOD.

I did. We called all the family in and she said her goodbyes. I called her best friend Mary who lived in Calgary as Gwen wanted her to come. She wanted to say goodbye to her and that her and Heine would be with me when she passed on. On the Friday night, Gwen got up to use the washroom while we were watching TV and said she was dizzy. I got up and helped her to the bathroom. As we turned the corner into the bedroom bathroom she fainted. Turning the narrow corner I did not have a good hold or a good balance and we both fell to the floor together with a crash, cut, bruised and bleeding we lay on the floor but the cuts did not hurt nearly as much as our hearts, as we lay crying on the floor in each others arms, finally realizing, **this WAS the end.**

Saturday morning the grand kids showed up and watched Saturday morning cartoons with Grandma in bed. Saturday afternoon Heine and Mary arrived and Mary and Gwen talked till late, with Gwen dozing off for a few hours now and then.

Saturday when I went to bed I prayed all night for GOD to have mercy and to take Gwen in her sleep tonight. She did NOT want to go to a hospice and I had promised I would not take her back to the hospital ever again after we did the "Big Escape" back a year or so before. I never slept that night but just lay there still, not wanting to disturb her, and pleading with GOD. At 3:00 am I got up to use the washroom and asked, no demanded that GOD take her before 6:00 am, **or else.**

I watched the clock.

At 6:00 am I could still hear Gwen's very shallow and strained breathing as it had been for months now. Tears rolled down my face as the clock passed 6:00 am and I turned to GOD and said I could not do a thing and it was only HIS will that would be done and surrendered my "must fix it" husband role.

At 6:05, Sunday morning of Sept 26, 2010, Gwen released a big breath and then stopped.

Her journey here on earth was over
and her new adventure in heaven had just begun.

77: EUTHANASIA ... Gwen Part II
on Gwen's death in Sept 26, 2010.

This is an addendum to the other story I wrote earlier, I glossed over what was really happening but feel now I need to say what was really going on that night.

In 1970, Gwen and I watched the movie **"They Shoot Horses Don't They ?".** The story is of a court case where a guy shoots his girlfriend after she asks him too to take her out of her suffering. In court his only defense is they shoot horses don't they? He recalls the story of his Grandfather shooting the beloved family horse which had broken a leg. He shoots it so it would not suffer.

Gwen and I discussed **the concept of euthanasia** and she stated she did not want to suffer, if she was dying, she asked me to euthanize her and not put her in a home or hospital to die a long and painful death.

My Grandmother spent about 8 years (?) in a nursing home bed slowly dying.

Gwen's Grandmother, **Nana, had died at about age 90**. She still lived on her own and had spent the week going out dining with some friends that were in town from Winnipeg for the week. After a week of partying she had a heart attack in her sleep and died. Now that is how to go out. That was January 1971 just a month after Gwen and I were married.

That was followed a few months later by Gwen's mother announcing she had cancer and was not expected to live 6 months. That Christmas after the big family dinner Gwen's Dad announced he had cancer too, with no hope of cure. Gwen's Mom died I think in the Spring of 1972, just 6 months after she was diagnosed as they had told her. We were living in Golden and they lived in Victoria.

We got the call to come and we drove. My little Datsun spent most of the time with it wheels in the air just to touch down on the road long enough for me to adjust the direction. We were going 100 miles an hour, literally. That would be 160 km to you younger folk.

We went thru a radar trap in the Rogers Pass but did not get stopped, I think the policemen saw it was a cheap rusted out old Datsun and figured his radar gun must be malfunctioning and no way he was going to call his pullover buddy down the road to say a Datsun just clocked at 100 mph going uphill. It is 500 miles from Golden to Vancouver and back then there was no Coquahalla, we just caught the ferry in time.

We went straight to the hospital and when we got there, Hilda, Gwen's Mom woke up and gave her a big hug. They chatted for about 15 minutes and we left for her Dad's house just down the street a few blocks. As we entered the house, the phone rang, it was the hospital, she had passed.

It has always amazed me how often, someone is dying is they are **able to hang on just long enough** to say that last goodbye and sometimes get permission to go. It upsets me greatly when I see how selfish some people are when a loved one is suffering and dying and the loved ones do not give them their blessing to move on.

The doctors had some better medication and they told her Dad, the Reverend (pastor) Robert that he would likely live 10 years. 10 years later almost to the day Gwen's Dad died. He was doing relieving pastor work in a church in Blue Creek, BC, north of Kamloops. He decided to leave as he wanted to go visit his brother in Seattle. His "senses" told him he had to go, that something was wrong and he had to go. Robert had chatted to me a few times about it and he mentioned he believed that he had like psychic powers and would get intuitions from time to time. He said they always came true.

As he was a pastor, I found it strange he called them intuitions and psychic power rather than that he talked to GOD and GOD told him. I guess that was just not said back then, kind of a church taboo. Too bad, what is the point of religion if you do not get that relationship with GOD ? I believe he had a great relationship with GOD, but was afraid to say it as that was not the custom of the church then, might be considered Pentecostal or something and likely lose his job as a freak.

Anyway, he made it to Vancouver and stayed overnight at his son Bob's house. He ended up in the hospital and again, we got the call to come quickly.

This was in 1982 and we lived in Comox, BC. Again we made it to the hospital and had a good chat. We took turns sitting with him, singing some of his favorite songs and reading some favorite verses. I was the last to sit with him as he passed away at about 3:00 am.

He had preached on Sunday at the church and then went out for lunch with folks before driving to Vancouver, then Weds he died. Quick and pretty much no suffering for which we were very thankful. His intuition was for his brother but ended up being for him. Also, I have always cautioned people on setting a date, like 6 months to live or 10 years. The body seems to listen to that talk and live accordingly. You are what you think. I read today that being happy isn't something you do, it is all about what you choose to think.

Also, Dad Young had made a few requests for his burial, such as where, who to speak, giving who things etc. He never told anyone he just put a letter in his top desk drawer to be found. Problem was, he died in Vancouver and we were all there so had a quick funeral and will reading and divided up the stuff. Gwen's dad was always worried about a big battle over his stuff. Very funny when you think about it as he was a very poor preacher with almost nothing. We agreed the things he had, if anyone wanted we would price and that would come off their inheritance. It worked perfect.

When Gwen went to clean out his house a few weeks later and found the letter, it was too late. I suggest you discuss with your executor, the job is hard enough without knowing all the facts and desires.

I remember I helped a friend with his fathers estate. He had every bank book and life insurance policy he ever owned. We spent six months contacting the banks and life insurance companies. Some insurance companies were gone and we had to find who took them over. No one would tell us anything until we sent them official documentation so they would not breach confidentiality. I think in the end, every bank account and every life insurance policy was closed.

I suggest everyone should give to their Executor a letter of what banks you deal at, where the will is, what life polices and real estate. You have entrusted them with a big job, please make it easier. You don't need to give dollar amounts if that bothers you but save the big search and make it easier for them. It is really hard to ask questions once you have died.

Back to the conversation: In 1988 **my Dad at age 80** had a few heart attacks and ended up in an old folks care home. We lived in Invermere, BC and came down for visit. When I entered the Care home my Dad was sitting in a wheelchair waiting for me. I walked right past him and down the hall to his room as I did not recognize him. He was a skeleton of the man he was, a mere shadow of his old self. My Dad was a big farmer turned construction man. 6'2" and likely 250 lbs of solid muscle. He would arm wrestle any man, even young steel workers, and always won.

After not seeing my Dad in his room I went back and he looked me in the eyes and I recognized the loving soul in those eyes. I wheeled him to the dining room as they were to be eating and he just sat there.
I asked if he wanted me to feed him and he just shook his head no. I told him he had to eat or he would die, with that he placed his hand on my hand and with tears in his eyes he said, "I know". He just wanted to die and move on.

He had had a number of strokes or heart attacks in the past few years and was almost not able to do anything for himself. He knew he was being a big burden on Mom and that she was getting worn out too. He had been in control all his life, Superintendent of large construction jobs, he called the shots. Now he was bathed, clothed, washed by others and a burden on those he loved. He had lived a long and adventurous life. I could remember he could quote hundreds of Bible verses from memory. He was a layman preacher, filling in here and there at churches. Normally his message would be a string of verses, which he would quote from memory with such authority. His favorite was:

I Corinthians 15: 51- 58

"Listen, I tell you a mystery: We will not all sleep, but we will all be changed in a flash, in the twinkling of an eye, at the last trumpet. For the trumpet will sound, the dead will be raised imperishable, and we will be changed. For the perishable must clothe itself with the imperishable, and the mortal with immortality. When the perishable has been clothed with the imperishable, and the mortal with immortality, then the saying that is written will come true: "Death has been swallowed up in victory.
Where, O death, is your victory?
Where, O death, is your sting?
The sting of death is sin, and the power of sin is the law.
But thanks be to God!
He gives us the victory through our Lord Jesus Christ.
Therefore, my dear brothers and sisters, **stand firm. Let nothing move you. Always give yourselves fully to the work of the Lord,** because you know that your labor in the Lord is not in vain."

****

My Dad believed this with all his heart and now he just wanted to live it. He starved himself to death.

He took control and made it happen, like he had always lived.

So you can see from my experiences, that in some cases, I believe in euthanasia.

That fateful night, as you read the other story of Gwen's death you will see where we come to midnight of Sept 25th 2010 and I have a promise to fulfill. I had promised Gwen that I would never put her in a home and that she would die in her own bed. She loved her bed. That I would at the right time help her move from this life to the next.

I had figured out how. Gwen was taking the oxicodon drug. That is the pain drug I believe Micheal Jackson overdosed and died on. She had started on 5 mg (or whatever size) and was now taking 100 mg pills. I would take a number of the 100 mg pills, crush them into a powder and dissolve them into a drink. The number of pills and fact that it was powder not a pill that dissolved over time would be sufficient. The doctor had warned me to keep those pills locked up because if anyone else took just one, who had not worked up their intake over time, they would die instantly.

From the previous story you will recall that Gwen had called me home on Tuesday and asked for to get all the kids and grandkids to come so she could say her goodbyes. Then asked me to call her best friend Mary and her husband to come out from Calgary to be there. They arrived on Saturday morning and they spent whatever time Gwen could stay awake talking.

That night I was helping Gwen to the bedroom and as we turned the corner, she lost consciousness for a second and fell. We were just turning the corner in a tight hallway and I was off balance and fell with her. We both fell to the floor with a crash against the wall and door. Bruised and cut but more broken hearted inside as we both realized as we lay there crying in each others arms that it was over.

I asked God to please take Gwen home in her sleep that night. **I gave God a deadline,** a literal deathline of 6:00 am Sunday. If HE did not take her by 6:00 I would take matters into my own hands and give her the drink and do as Gwen had asked and we agreed, "they kill horses when they are suffering and will not recover don't they ?"

Surely we should have more mercy on the ones we love.

I had laid there all night pleading in anguish with GOD and listening to Gwen's breath. The 6:00 am deadline came and went and nothing had been done. It was time to take matters into my own hand and get the job done. I got up at 6:04 to get the drink and suffered thru the long walk from the washroom where it was to the bed. I lamented but could not do it. I dumped the drink into the sink and cried out to GOD to please help and just take Gwen now as I could not do it. **I needed GOD !** I crawled in anguish back into bed and settled in just to hear Gwen take one last big breath, then silence.

She had moved on, like she had asked, in her own bed with no pain and surrounded by her best friends.

Thank you Lord ...

78: Living to 60 Or 120 in 2011

Many times I heard Gwen say she would only live to 60. Her Mom
died at 60 and I think her brother did too. I begged her many times
not to talk like that as I believe the body does not know the
difference between reality and thought. If the mind tells it to do it, it
just does it.

I read in the Bible the other day around Noah's time that GOD said
he would limit man to 120 years, I told GOD I would hold him to the
120 years and revised my retirement plan to 2050, at age 119 I will
retire so I get one year in retirement before I leave this mortal shell
and my spirit moves onto eternity.
(I thought we needed a short happy story after that last few)

79: A GIFT from GOD x

The time from Gwen getting sick to my emotional recovery was
about five years. Five years before that I had left the banks and
started my own business. I was able to do that as we got a generous
buy out in 1998 from a bank and then a double buyout from TD bank
in 2002. In 2007 some friends in the business and I looked at
making a partnership so we could cover for each other when one was
away. We were in the process when Gwen got sick. I delayed but
then on a labour day weekend Gwen asked me to make the move.
She would feel better knowing I was with my business partners
rather than alone when she was gone.

I went into negotiations and the company we were wanting to deal
with us offered some money to join up. I was expecting moving my
office expenses but they offered sufficient for 3 years wages, I was
shocked. They took the look on my face that I was insulted and
immediately offered 5 years for a five year contract.
I signed!

What a GOD send. 5 years of the wages, so I could stay home and
look after Gwen and still get paid. Two banks paid me to get lost
and now these guys were paying me to come.

GOD's timing is perfect.!!

80: WHEN I WALKED Thru the VALLEY of the SHADOW of DEATH. In 2011

To anyone who has just suffered the loss of a loved one... I share my experience trusting it will give you hope and ask you to continue to walk your life's journey path.

30 months as caregiver to my wife of almost 40 years was nothing compared to the winter alone after her passing. Her death was anticipated as she was diagnosed terminal in 2008 and I thought I had come to terms with it all and once the journey of Caregiver was over, I would move easily into my new role and new life. Gwen died on Sept 26, 2010.

Here is an excerpt from my diary, dated April 1, 2011

"It seems like these six months being alone were a lot harder than the three years with cancer and Gwen's death. I have described it like being a ship without a rudder. I do have a full 2010 to 2050 life plan with a mission statement, purpose and even specific actions, all those great things, **but all these are worthless if you have no desire.**

The feeling is much more than just limbo, it is more like walking along a dark and desolate valley trail. You are perched on this ledge, walking slowly and carefully while taking time to stop and look over the side to a bottomless chasm of depression. It would be so easy to slip into that chasm of self-pity, depression and lack of will or care. I know that this is a time that I need to keep slowing walking the valley trail as I know that in time, I will reach a spot where I can exit this valley and go back into the sunlight. "

After writing that I joined a golf club and golfed everyday from April to August. I got fresh air, exercise and met new people. Also got my handicap down from a 16 to a scratch on a big course. Interesting there were 5 other guys who had just lost their wives that winter and were wandering aimlessly around the golf course too, trying to find their way.

81: SOS to GODx in 2011

After my wife had died, I found the winter nights to be the worst. Dark and cold and very bored and alone. One night I awoke and was grieving almost in pain and I cried out to GOD please help. I looked at the clock and it was 5:05, what I saw was SOS. Your SOS has been received and help is on its way.

Much later after Patricia and I were married, one night I woke and saw the time was 2:02, What I saw was a reverse SOS which said to me help had arrived. It definitely had.

Thank you GOD.

82: A Christmas Dime Story. Dec 2010

Dec 11,2010. A Christmas story that will bring a tear to your eye and Hope to heart.

A busy Saturday getting ready for Christmas. Alot of running around picking up presents and cleaning the house getting ready for Christmas parties and friends. I stopped by my office to drop off some boxes from my trunk to make room as I needed to pick up some presents. Very much out of the way but thought I should as I had forgotten to take them out at home. I noticed a package on my desk. It was from our dear friends Heine & Mary. Inside was a wrapped Christmas present, but then I saw "the card".

This is not just any card, this is a very special card. For as many years as I can remember Heine & Mary and Gwen & I, almost 30 years had exchanged the same card. Actually, there are two cards, one we sent to them, the other they sent to us, then vice versa the next year. We would write what had happened that year, our visits, our trips together, our Children and Grandchildren, our memories, some bad, mostly good. The following year we dated it and add comments to the card we have and return it. Thereby the two cards go back and forth and you not only get to read what they wrote, but alternatively what each other wrote in previous years, back to when the kids were babies.

But this was not that card.

It was a new card, with no history, no memories, and no Gwen. I burst into tears as the reality of it all hit home. Maybe the first time since Gwen died some 2 months before I truly grieved.

I started for home. I needed gas but decided not to go to my usual station as it was the old right turn to home and I now go left. I drove and found a station on my new route. Filled up with a pay at the pump but decided I needed a Pepsi. Why pay for Pepsi I thought, you have lots in the fridge at home, you can wait and you don't need it.

But I went in anyway and bought the $0.99 Pepsi which came to $1.11 The young man behind the counter was in a very festive, talkative and good mood. I was having a hard time holding back my tears as he tried to chat up a storm.

All I had was a $20 so he said I'll take a penny from the give/take jar and even up the change to 18.90 back. He gave me three $5's, a Toonie, a Loonie, three Quarter , a nickel and "**a Dime**". But he only commented on the dime. He held the dime up in a "Derylize" dramatic like a carnival man said "This lucky dime. For you sir, this very worn and old but historic DIME. It is a 1979 dime, do you know anything that happened in 1979 ?" That was long before he was born. I said yes, choking back my tears as I left the gas station. Yes, 1979 is when we meet the Larsens and we started the special Christmas Cards. It was some time before I could drive just taking all that had just happened.

But what is so significant about a dime. Gwen and I always joked that when anything was going wrong, we would find a dime in the weirdest places. Gwen always said that her Mom had sent her that dime to remind her that she was with her and all would be OK. Her Mom died in 1972 and we have storage full of dimes found in unexplainable places all at key times, especially these last three years as she battled cancer.

Read this again, and you tell me. Did Gwen or maybe GOD have that young man under great fanfare, give me that 1979 dime to let me know all is OK? There is no question in my mind. It was good to get that real first burst of tears and to remember all the good memories we have as written in those cards, but also to cherish the memories we are making this Christmas with family and friends, and even a strange friendly young man at the gas station who has no idea how he made this Christmas very special, to me.

83: BEST GOLF EVER! In 2010
A walk in the dark with My HEAVENLY FATHER.

Golfing in the dark with no glasses and I shot my best game ever.

Gwen's friend Rhonda from Vancouver stayed over to be with Gwen for awhile as she was dying from cancer. I decided to take some time for myself as I had been a caregiver for a number of years now. I went golfing at Mission Creek Golf Course in Kelowna, an executive course just to spend some quiet time with myself and have a chat with GOD.

Just as I was heading out I lost the screw in my glasses, so I left them at home. I can't see the ball more than about 50 feet without my glasses so would have to golf basically blind. So I said, OK GOD, I'll try and hit the ball the best I know how and you watch it for me. I played the best game of my life.

The first 9 holes it was light but the sun set around hole 6. By the time I got to hole 14 it was dark with only light was from the city giving me sufficient light to see where I needed to go and where to hit.

Hole 5, 307 yds, with 3 very large willows that are between the tee and the green making it a dog leg right. You need to either go over the trees which was very difficult as you need a perfect shot and high or hit a perfect fade shot, as needs to start left and then fade right around the trees. The problem is the fairway is about 200 ft wide at the 200 yd point, but then as it turns right, it gets down to about 20 ft wide in front of the green, a some 300 yd drive.

I hit my ball, no idea where it went. I wandered down the fairway looking at my usual spots either under the willows if it gets caught by the branches and then over to left in the deeper grass if it went straight.

I was ready to give up looking (as I didn't have my glasses on) and was heading for the next tee box when I looked right in front of the green and there was the ball, just short of the green, on the very narrow fairway. I gasped in unbelief, amazement and thankful.

Hole 14, 270 yds. I've never hit this green before,(over 100 rounds played on that course and this was the crow hole too) usually to the right under/behind the willows. I hit, felt good but no idea as I never saw a thing. I hit a second just in case. I wandered up the fairway doing a sweeping walking back and forth as I could only see 10 to 20 feet around me, looking to my usually landing spot under the willow on the right, no balls, started to walk to the 15th tee and crossed the 14th very small green on my way. There was one of my ball 20 feet from the cup. I gasped outloud, very loud, in shock. Then I looked at the cup to see how far it was to putt, and there about 3 feet from the cup was my other ball.

Same story on hole 15 being 237 yards, shorter, but you need to cross a large pond just before the green.

Same story on hole 16 being 207 yds, and very protected by big willows and other large trees that I have never successfully got over, around or thru to get to the green. The fairway between them is very narrow. I hit two balls again as I was not sure. Both were only feet from the cup. I have never hit this green before either. Again when I saw them and I gasped and fell to my knees in amazement, gasped so loud I am sure they heard me downtown.

Hole 18, hit 2 balls into the dark, where they went I have no idea. I know I did not hit them well so they likely went out of bounds into the trees. They turned the sprinklers on so I was just going to go to the car but I had to walk past the green on the way to the car just in case and you guessed it, one ball was on the apron of the green, the other I knew had gone into the trees, but then I saw the other ball just on the side of green against the tall grass, but a very makeable shot.

I figure GOD sent me for 18 perfect holes of which I had 8 easy birds. I only made one bird as I could not see the curves on the greens. (my excuse and I am sticking to it). I ended up 5 over because of my putting but had a shot at being 8 under..... I have lost likely 50 balls on that course as it is narrow and a lot of water. That day I went home with my "play ball".

Best of all it was an awesome walk in the dark with our Father.

The next day I went out again in the daylight. Keep in mind a few months before I was a 16 handicapper, which means on a good day, I would golf 16 shots over par. This is was a par 62 course.

That day, I was 7 under coming to the last hole and had never had even a par game before. I was so nervous not to ruin it on the last hole I duffed my tee shot. The ball went out about 10 yards on this 100 yd par 3. Oh no, so I took out my faithful 8 iron and just wanted to bump and run it onto the green to be safe. It got onto the green hit the pin and dropped into the cup and I fell to my knees in unbelief. I was 8 under, 8 being my favorite number as I am the 8th son.

(Those who know the course, I started on hole 2 that day, so my #18 was the normal hole #1.)

84: My Easter Dream

Last night I had a dream and I had blood on my hands.
Strange...

I looked for signs of a cut, but could not find any.
I washed my hands.
Then my hands and arms were all covered in blood.
I washed that and was getting frantic.
Do I need to go to a Doctor, as I could see no source?
In a panic, I washed my arms and hands and immediately my whole
body was covered in blood.
Was this a sign that I had some terrible disease, or what was it all
about.............

Then I heard GOD speak to me.

"No my Son, I just wanted you to know that you have been washed
in the blood of the Lamb, My Son, Jesus Christ. Your sins that were
scarlet are now as white as snow; you have been washed in the blood
of the Lamb." You are forgiven.

NOW THAT'S A BAPTISM............

85: A FLEECE as to WHERE does GOD want me to SERVE NOW ? in 2011

I am searching for where the Lord wishes me to serve. This is the story of the amazing journey that leads me to where I am to serve at KGF, Kelowna Gospel Fellowship Church at Gordon & Casorso in Kelowna.

Now that I am single and need something to pour myself into, what do I do? Back just after Gwen died, I woke up and the clock said 3:00 am. Wide wake, Ok GOD, you want to chat. 3:00 am seems to be the time GOD likes to schedule meetings or maybe it is I am too busy all day so HE lets me get some sleep, then wakes me at 3:00. This has happened more times than I can count and I am not complaining as they are usually, no always, awesome meetings. I told GOD, I want to make sure that I don't just jump into something to fill my loneliness, but rather that it is YOUR will, YOUR plan for what I am to do. So here is the deal. I believe I am looking at going into men's ministry and warm welcoming church to fit my life and make true friends.

Therefore, if I go to a church and I get invited out for coffee or lunch by 2 men and the pastor, different times, that will be my fleece.

The fleece I am referring to was when in the Bible someone was looking for a sign from GOD to do something, first he put the fleece (a sheep skin) out and it was to be dry in the morning but the ground damp with dew. Then he did it and the ground was to be dry and fleece wet. GOD did it and so the person had his sign that this was GOD's will for that person.

I have gone to many churches in the town over the past 5 months. Mostly I believe I was not mentally ready for any commitment yet. Last Thurs, I got my act together and here we go.

I had been going to Kamloops on the weekends and wanted to stay overnight to attend my old church, Summit Drive (Baptist). Each week it didn't work out and I drove home Saturday. Last Saturday I decided to take a couple out to the Keg for supper and stay overnight and attend the church.

My usual place I stay was able to take me but they had their two married children, with babies staying overnight for the weekend too. So I declined.

I got an email from Aldon, Chris, my son's father-in-law. He said that pastor Mike of Kelowna Fellowship Church (KGF) wanted to get in touch with me and could he give him my email and phone. Actually he had given him my business card as I had just given the card to Aldon at Mikaya's birthday party (our mutual granddaughter) a few days ago, where Aldon and I had a really good chat. Not about this, but other stories Aldon was telling me.

I thought rather than going to Summit Drive church I would head home and go meet this pastor Mike. Now why was he looking for me? Aldon had mentioned to me that he had a meeting with this pastor, so I jokingly said, say Hi to him for me. Aldon looked at me and said "do you know him?", I said no, but I have meet him, ask him if he remembers the guy with the hat on the Christmas Eve service who said, "I'm just casing the joint". He did and he did.

So I went to the church on Sunday morning. When I entered the church, I was greeted at the door by Jake, the door welcomer. He and many others gave me a warm welcome. I wandered around, still casing the joint, and Jake came running after me, told me he was very busy at the door right now but made me promise that **I would not leave** until he had a chance to talk with me. Sure. In my wanderings I bumped into the pastor in a back hallway, he was going somewhere and gave a smile and polite hi, but need to be somewhere, understandable, it was almost "showtime".

I noticed in the bulletin and the pastor mentioned from the pulpit that they were looking at starting a ministry to the " Boomers". My age group. Anyone 55-69 yrs old interested was to meet at 11:45 for coffee and discussion in the fellowship room. Service ended about 11:15 so had time to blow. Wandered around and found they had after church coffee and desserts in their gym. Chatted with a number of people. Somewhere I started talking to a guy named Helmut. He was a realtor. He kind of attached himself to me and we had good chats. I ended having to say I had to go as I was attending the "Boomers Meeting".

I wandered over, found a chair near the back far side so I wouldn't take over and said I would just listen. A gorgeous energetic passionate young (qualified as a Boomer) women with flowing full gorgeous hair sat in front of me. She appeared to be very interested in the ministry. Wow I thought, maybe I might start looking at women sooner than I thought. As she talked and engaged herself into the meeting, I kept trying to see if she had a ring on her finger. Though she moved her hands around a lot in her energetic speaking I could not see. Helmet came and sat beside me. We exchanged business cards.

When the meeting was done, pastor Mike gave out some books on "Baby Boomer Ministry", he ran out of books but told people he had more coming in a few weeks. After everyone had got up and had their say with the Pastor, he saw me standing behind some people in the corner, came over and said, I just wanted to introduce myself as I don't think I know your name. I said, in my smart Alex way, "actually, you know my name, you just don't know me, I am Deryl Priebe, I understand you are looking for me". Well, his eyes lit up and he grabbed me by the arm and said I just had to come to his office. We went to his office and he gave me his own book on the baby boomers. He said read this and then we will do coffee or lunch.

I left, bumped into Helmut at the door and he asked what I was doing for lunch, I said nothing , so he invited me to join him, his wife and 3 other couples. Great luncheon. His wife was beside him and he introduced me to her. She was that gorgeous energetic passionate young woman with flowing hair. OK, take her off my list as she is taken. You're a lucky man Helmut.

Oh, I had walked to my car and had to come back as I remembered I had promised Jake I would not leave without talking to him. Also to tell Helmut that I would be a little late as I had promised Jake I would chat with him before I left. He was doing some counselling upstairs, I had wandered into that meeting already, so I went up and gave him my card and apologized that I had to go as was doing lunch with some people. He said he had only wanted to invite me out for coffee sometime this week if I was available.

I asked him, were you the guy that called me a number of times about 3 years ago and invited me out and I never got back to you. That was when Gwen & I had first attended that church, the Sunday the last pastor resigned. He said yes, it was him. I apologize for not getting back to him but that I wrote his number down, but Gwen had just been diagnosed with cancer and I just didn't want to talk. So 3 yrs late, but we did coffee on Tuesday.

Pastor Mike and I are doing lunch the next Tuesday, earliest possible date with alot of juggling to make work. So, you look at these coffee or luncheons, none just happened. One was 3 years late, another was from curiosity of comments I am assuming made by the associated pastor to the pastor on the guy with hat that was just casing the joint and he managed to get my name as Aldon, who I had a long chat with at our mutual granddaughter birthday party had mentioned he was having lunch with that pastor. I jokingly said to ask if he remembered me and he did and thereby got my name. And Helmut, how I bumped into a number times that Sunday, even after I had left for my car but had to come back as I promised Jake I would not leave.

So, within a few minutes of each other, basically , but totally separate conversations and reasons, Jake, Helmut and Pastor Mike, all asked me out for coffee or lunch. My fleece is filled, I was to attend KGF.

Since that time many things have happened which I will discuss in other stories. Key things:

1) Helmut is now one of my best friends.

2) I have since married and when Jake invited my new bride and me to his house for dinner one night, it turns out his wife and my new wife went to high school together, that was in Abbotsford two hundred miles away.

3) I told Pastor Mike, 'It is time". It is time to get serious about KGF's Men's Ministry. We launched the next Sunday, Father's day, with the movie "courageous". To be the men, the fathers, the husbands, the friends: WE SHOULD BE.

86: OUR LOVE STORY"
Patricia and Deryl "Our Love Story"
Written for our wedding on January 21, 2012.

Welcome and thank you so much for sharing this special day with us. Patricia and I have had a whirlwind fairy tale kind of romance and knew the first time we met... we had met our soul mate. **"It feels like home, to me."** Those are the words of our song and it expresses how we felt from the first phone call to how we feel today. **"Home."** One of the most beautiful words. A word, a feeling, a place, an expression that you are comfortable, loved, wanted, appreciated, safe and in peace. All wrapped up in one word. I believe we all long for that place to call home, I know we did.

Our life circumstances and how we deal with them make us who we are. Patricia went through her battle with breast cancer, accompanied by unemployment (as she could not work) and a leaky condo. I had spent the past few years as a caregiver to my wife Gwen who had since died from cancer. *We chose to rejoice for each day for our friends, our family and our strong faith.*

We would like to share some of our story with you and trust you will be encouraged by it.

On a warm Okanagan August day, after forty years, Patricia and Deryl met over lunch. It seemed only minutes into the luncheon as we chatted and looked into each other's souls and realized that we had found our destiny. By the end of the luncheon it was felt the search was over, **life was to begin.**

The next date we sat on a park bench by the lake at Peachland and asked every question imaginable. Later, dinner at Manteo Resort on the deck by the lake right at sunset. Then we strolled along the promenade by the Grand Hotel under the August moonlight, I said to Pat, **"no holding hands and no kissing !"** as I did not want to get my emotions distorting my inquiry . Later when I was telling my son Chris the story, he said, "Dad, you seem to be treating this like a job interview, maybe you should try some romance."

The next date, I told Pat that the rules about "no holding hands and no kissing" were now gone…. I took her into my arms and we kissed. We had a beautiful walk in the woods down to the river. We shared our life stories and dreams. I told a story of how I had an imaginary friend when I was young, just someone to talk to when I went for long walks alone in the woods. Her name was Heather. She told me her full name is <u>Heather</u> Patricia Mae. It was like I had finally met my childhood friend again, now in person.

Chris, my son, asked if we might be cousins. (That boy asked too many questions.) **No!** Well, she is from Clearbrook, Mennonite heritage and her last name is Schmidt as was my Grandmother's. We looked into it and we do share the same Great, Great Grandparents. Also, the first time I went to visit Patricia at her place it looked familiar, turns out Patricia Schmidt's apartment is now on the property where my Grandma Schmidt's house was.

It all started with an email on July 2 from Pat asking if I had some old college pictures as Pat and Gwen were college roommates back at Briercrest in 1969. Pat was trying to put a picture book together of her life and did not have any of that era. (That is her story and she is sticking to it) Rather than emailing Pat back, I decided to call. Nothing like a little off guard call to have some fun. The call was so comfortable for both, it was like two old friends just chatting, amazing after 40 years. I asked if she wanted to do lunch when she was up in Kelowna in late August and Pat agreed.

Pat's friend Tina told her, this is more than a date; this one is for real, trust me. I wrote in my journal a few days before the date ***"Is this GOD's choice for my workmate? Kind of a pre-arranged marriage?*** Funny thing, I was not looking, well, saying I wasn't anyway. I had grown a scraggy beard as I just got back for a sailing trip with buds to Desolation Sound and didn't shave. I kept the beard, thought it would scare off the women…. Pat loved it.

We say we believe that GOD prearranged our marriage and ***<u>guided our lives</u>***, what do we mean by this? Pat's first email was inspired by the fact that my name kept coming up and just felt she needed to contact me.

I mistook her for another Pat from Vancouver I know. I did not want to connect with that other Pat so I avoided her.

First, there was a situation at work that required Pat to take some debriefing. The person she was sent to see was Ross Priebe. She asked and sure enough, he was Deryl's nephew. My brother Lloyds middle son. Then another of her friends commented that their son worked with Deryl's sons. Another friend commented that she was a Priebe before she got married and was Deryl's 1st cousin. The big one was when a co-worker showed her the picture of the dream house she had bought to retire in at Kelowna and invited Pat to come up. Pat right away realized that it was Gwen's dream house and that Deryl must have sold it to her. So many little items **she just could not ignore, nor could I.**

On my side, I was working on my 2010-2050 life plan. The key was to continue to work with men in relationship building. Women do this well for supporting each other, men don't. I was working on listing all the various things I needed and then realized I had some major shortfalls and would need some guys to come along side to pick up the slack. I only got three of my shortfalls jotted down when the phone rang and I didn't get back to it.
I figured I knew who would fit that job perfectly to do those things and gave him a call to have coffee. He said he was just getting into his camper and heading out for a month.

At our first luncheon on August 22, I asked Pat what she had done when she was overseas. Pat answered calmly but verbatim the three shortfalls I had listed. …. I was dumbfounded at her comment and realized that this was not just a normal luncheon, but was likely a major piece to my life plan, and that Pat, Patricia as I call her, as Pat is too simple for such a blessing. Then GOD showed up and told my Spirit, **She is my Gift to you.** I asked what I should call her, Pat or Patricia, whichever she said, I said Pat is too simple for such a glorious gift, I thereafter will call you Patricia.

Shortly after Patricia told me the three things she did overseas, she let me know that she had had cancer, breast cancer. In 2004 she had undergone major surgery.

I had made a note in my life plan that if any women appeared in anyway sickly or especially if they had cancer, I was to exit the building immediately. I had just spent almost four years as a caregiver to Gwen as she lost her battle with cancer. But I was at total peace with Patricia telling me about her cancer. If GOD had gone to all this effort to bring us together, I was not going to let a simple cancer situation concern me.

For me, the 30 months as caregiver was nothing compared to the winter alone. I will repeat the excerpt from my diary, dated April, 2011. *"It seems like these six months being alone were a lot harder than the three years with cancer and Gwen's death. I have described it like being a ship without a rudder. I do have a full 2010 to 2050 life plan with mission statement, purpose and even specific actions, all those great things,* ***but all these are worthless if you have no desire.*** *The feeling is much more than just limbo, it is more like walking along a dark and desolate valley trail. You are perched on this ledge, walking slowly and carefully while taking time to stop and looking over the side to a bottomless chasm of depression. It would be so easy to slip into that chasm of self-pity, depression and lack of will or care. I know that this is a time that I need to keep slowing walking the valley trail as I know that in time, I will reach a spot where I can exit this valley and go back into the sunlight. "*

Patricia brought me out of that valley into a radiate light. People say that we glowwww. And even more, music has returned to my life. For the past four years I listened to no music, now tears of joy flow down my checks in <u>peaceful joy as</u> I again listen to my favourite pieces.

So, how do you know when to make a commitment? **A commitment to someone is for life**. For me, marriage is a life vow. If you don't believe in your lifetime commitment, sometimes you look for an easy way out, instead of resolving. For me, I needed a sign from GOD. I had already asked for many and got them but what I needed was a clincher, because I was thinking of asking Patricia to marry me, and you know what I think of that commitment, lifetime, so I had to be sure.

So I said to GOD, "GOD, I cannot figure out any sign so wondrous that I would unquestionably believe it. I will leave it to YOU to create a sign so BIG that there will be no question that this is what I am to do." **He did and did it bigger, so grandiose, so timely and so *Deryl specific* that I will never again question, that this relationship is of GOD.**

87: FINAL FLEECE (or sign) that I was to ask PATRICIA to marry me AFTER JUST 4 DATES.

To marry or not to marry Patricia, how do you know the answer to that question?

My wife had just died the Sept before and I was wondering if I was on the rebound or really in love. Was it my choice or GOD telling me this was the person HE had chosen for me. I had decided when I became a widower that I was not going to date for two years and then take five years before I married. Now I was in a serious relationship in one year and believing that I was going to ask her to marry me. It was all so quick and sudden, **but seemed so right**.

I was thinking we needed to spend more time together so I wanted to ask Patricia to quit her job, retire and move up to Kelowna from Abbotsford and move into my condo. I live on the acreage and the condo on the lake was vacant. It had been booked all summer by numerous friends and relatives but coinceditially would be vacant with no more bookings after Thanksgiving, just when I needed it. I could not ask her to quit her job, leave her family and friends and move 333 km (exact distance from her house to mine) if I was not willing to make some kind of a commitment. So, I needed to propose to show my commitment but after only four dates was I really ready and was this the right decision, *for sure.*

The curves in life's road don't always come as we plan them, so if this was GOD's plan as it was way too soon for me, I would need an **unquestionable sign from HIM**. I talked with GOD and told HIM, "I cannot figure out what kind of sign (or fleece as it is called) that I would unquestionably believe and not just looking for another sign as I had many answered signs already." So I told GOD HE was to come up with the fleece and make it so grand that there would be no question. I have used fleeces many times before when a major change in my life was to take place.

The biggest so far was when I took over the Cumberland Boys Club that story is totally unbelievable if I had not lived it. But this time I needed a very special one. GOD has always taken me at my word and exceeded any expectation. Here it is.

I was sitting at my computer in Sept 2011 composing an email to Patricia, thinking on what I could say to get her to move up to Kelowna so we could spend more time together and not have to drive the Coquahala through all the winter mountain highway conditions. I was not getting anywhere with my email so I turned the TV on. I couldn't find anything I liked. I went thru all my 899 or so satellite channels, **nothing.** I tried my PVR, after all, it had hours of shows I had picked as I wanted to watch them. **Nothing.**

Finally I just picked one of the Gathier Gospel Hours at random. (funny, the Gaithier hour just came on my TV again right now as I am writing this)I had the TV on music but I had scheduled the PVR to tape the Gather hour each Friday at 7:00pm so it just flipped over as I must be taping 2 things right now. I have been trying to sit down and write this blog for weeks and just hit this part of the story right now, go figure.)

The Gathier Gospel Hour had Sandy Patty as a quest on the one I picked at random out of the dozen I had taped. She was telling her life story to Bill and all the troubles she had been going thru, then she said, "You know Bill, I am just so happy...." I said to the TV out loud, 'So Sandy, what do you have to be so happy about, in my opinion you have really screwed up your life." Then she said again, **" I am so happy, because ..."**

I need to back up here and give you some history so this will all make sense.

Back in Sept 1993 I was taking my son Chris to Three Hills Prairie Bible School for his grade 12. We needed to send our son away for school as he had done the right thing by defending an innocent youth who was being bullied by a gang. The police advised me I had to get him out of town as he was marked by the gang and the RCMP rightfully feared for his life. Their fear was justified.

Anyway, the old car was loaded to the gunnels with all of Chris's books, computers and things. I was amazed it made it all the way from Kelowna over the mountains to Three Hills in Alberta. I dropped him off and did a quick turnaround as I had was running some seminars the next day back in BC.
I was only 30 minutes down the road when my engine went up in smoke. I pulled over into a field as I was on a side road and glory hallelujah I was about 100 yards from an old Ma and Pa gas station/restaurant. They could not help but had a tow truck and agreed to tow the car to the nearest GM dealer, which luckily was in Three Hills.

The school at Three Hills where Chris was offered to put me up while the repairs were being done. I made sure the repair guy was fully aware that *I was a very important man* as I was the Senior Consultant for a major bank and needed to have my car fixed ASAP as I had places to go and seminars and workshops to address for new Financial Planners. He calmly looked across the counter and said, **"You listen to me, City boy,** you say another word telling me what I have to do in **MY shop** and I will have your car towed back out onto the road and you can deal with it. You see all those trucks and other farm implements in the back, it is harvest time and my clients, who are my neighbours, and lifelong clients and friends, need me to fix them so they can harvest, so their families can eat. I will fix your car when I fix your car. I will try and have you on the road by next weekend. It was Monday."

I realized he was right and decided to take this week as an opportunity to think my life through. Better said, GOD really gave me no choice.

88: IS THERE REALLY A GOD ?

Is there really a God?

For days I lay back on the wide open prairie and looked out over the waiving grain to the Rocky Mountains in the distance. I remembered all the mountains I had climbed and the unbelievable majesty of creation that I witnessed. I looked up at night and saw the innumerable stars.

Infinitely and/or Eternity, words that I cannot comprehend. So just because I cannot comprehend it does not mean that it does not exist. It is like my 5th Grade class when the teacher drew a line on the chalk board and wrote the number "0". He then asked where the numbers ended, at a million? At a billion ? No matter where he drew the end line, there were still numbers on the other side, an infinite amount of numbers. He then showed the negative numbers going the other way. He did the same, no end. So infinite does exist even if I cannot comprehend it.

Infinite and eternity must exist because if it does not and the start and end are just time warped, then what is outside of that… **Call it nothing or call it eternity or call it GOD! It is something**. *I cannot explain, but the existence of a GOD actually makes the most logical answer.*

It is one thing to explain how the stars and sun work, it is harder to explain the complexities like my finger moving to pick up a dime, but how do you explain the creation of something like love or thought?

GOD, whatever that word means, provides the ability to create all that was created in its awesome complexity. I don't care if GOD did it by evolution from the Big Bang in a trillion years or Creation in 6 days. That does not matter to me. The only undeniable point is **something happened to create all we see and have today.**

So, for me, yes, **GOD is the most logical answer.**

89. *Does GOD CARE about ME ?*

My next question after I concluded there must be a GOD was, does GOD care about me, or did HE just create all things and let it run on its own. A Mother Nature like type god. By the way, I do not believe GOD is a "HE" but rather a Spirit. I understand there is no gender in heaven but that is another whole issue that seems to just divert us from seeking the real truth. Also, I have no comprehension of what a "Spirit" really is, especially one that is everywhere and all knowing.

So, after I thought all of this thru, it made the most logical sense. Yes, there is a GOD.

But again, does GOD really care about me. HE must, otherwise why would HE have made things so amazing. The whole universe is so planned that only a caring Being that cares for its own creation makes sense.

I was sitting on a picnic table at the time and a little sparrow came and I shared my sandwich with him. Then from nowhere I remembered the song, "His eye is on the sparrow, and I know He watches (cares for) me." **This was a life changing moment for me as I then believed that the Creator GOD did care for me.**

Since that time, I have documented hundreds of unbelievable stories, from the parting of clouds, healing a dying friend to complex assignments of doing good. Many are in this book but hardly a scratch of all I have experienced but more important, I have learned how to have a loving and caring relationship with GOD.

The greatest compliment I ever got was when a friend who said, "You're like Tevye from Fiddler on the Roof, no big deal, you just talk to GOD like you talk to me." Wow, I love it.

This whole process took me most of the week as my car was ready on Friday and so was I.

I was ready to move on with my relationship with GOD.

.

90: HEARING GOD'S VOICE:
Pray without ceasing.   I Thess 5:16

This Bible verse used to baffle me but turned out to be a key learning for me on developing my relationship with GOD.

When I first studied this concept I wondered how you could pray without ceasing. I was taught that when you pray, you bow your head, close your eyes and that the best prayers were done when you knee down in the quiet of your closest. This comes from a lot of different ideas and reasons why this is best but like so many thing that are taught and become "law or rules" are not properly interpreted.

There is a place for that quiet time with GOD but this verse says to pray without ceasing. When I am at work, when I am driving my car… how can I ?

So what is prayer? I concluded that Prayer is simply communicating or a word we use when talking to GOD. OK, that is better, we are to be in communication or relationship with GOD all the time, like HE is always with us, wherever we are or whatever we are doing.   That makes sense.

The other thing then is communication needs to be a two way street. Many Christians I have heard using their quiet time or devotional time to read the bible and they say GOD speaks to them thru HIS word.   I have a problem with that, yes I believe it is true and GOD has spoken to me that way, but I have problems with reading, focus really, I am little ADHD or as my son says, ADHHHHHHD and dyslectic. The words and letters move around and if you ever want to have a good laugh just have me read out loud, it can get really funny.

For me, prayer is more like when I had my imaginary friend Heather as a child.   I just carry on an ongoing conversation.   I hear lots of voices talking back in my head but have learned to differentiate them from GOD, my own thoughts and thoughts said from the enemy.

Is the other voice being negative and putting me down or trying to stop me from doing good works? That voice I need to take every thought into control and shut it down.

The rest of that "pray without ceasing" verse helps..." Rejoice always, pray without ceasing, give thanks in all circumstances; for this is the will of God in Christ Jesus for you."

Another voice which I hear is either my common sense or I call the Holy Spirit, I believe. It is hard for me to differentiate between the two, but they are good.

The third voice I hear only comes once and awhile. Most of them and nearly every conversation is in this book. I believe these are the voice of GOD my Heavenly Father. I never know when it will happen, I can be in a quiet place worshiping or normally doing something like driving my car, but when it comes, I know it. This is GOD as a spirit talking to my Spirit. When HE shows up my Spirit knows HIS voice and the hair on my neck stands on end while my eyes tear up with joy and excitement. My Spirit wants to just leap out of this body and join HIM .

GOD is usually short and abrupt with a very important message.

91: BACK to the FLEECE

The next time I remember hearing this song " His Eye is on the Sparrow" was when Chris and I were attending an Easter Service in Russia. His Mom and I were very worried when Chris told us that he was going to spend a year teaching in Russia. He was only 19. Then when we found out he was going to Krasnodar, our anxiety heightened, as that was only miles from the Chechnya boarder where a civil war was underway at that time. While Chris was there a nurse from Vancouver was killed. Also, one night the republic he was in declared independence from Russia and the police came and interigagated him until the wee hours of the morning. I believe they did not want this "Westerner" in their new country. You have already read more of this story which has some amazing things like how I got 2 full suitcases of Bibles thru customs without any detection and when we came across armed Russian soldiers standing shoulder to shoulder blocking our access to the Orthodox Church at Easter that we were about to attend.

Anyway, back to the point, we were in this church service in Russia and I was worrying about him, when they sang that song. I looked around me and saw the church elders sitting at the front on stage, they looked like apple doll faces with their very rugged faces, definitely had had hard long lives. I thought what their lives must have been like over the past 70 years compared to mine. I had nothing to complain about, I was blessed. And I knew, GOD was telling me HE cared for the little sparrow and that HE was watching over Chris, even in the far off plains of Russia. It gave me peace.

The next time I remember hearing the song I sitting on my couch the winter after my wife had died. It was one of those long and lonely winter nights. I was watching a TV special of an Alaskan Cruise, and this lady came on and sang that song. I knew then that spring was coming and better days were ahead.

So, for me, yes, a caring GOD is the most logical answer. If I am wrong, no harm, but it has been an unbelievably exciting ride believing in GOD guiding and leading me and the amazing and unexplainable things HE has done in my life. Also to have that faith thru both the troubled and awesome times makes my life worthwhile day by day.

Now back to the final fleece as I sat working on my email to Patricia and questioning why Sandy Patty was so happy. Then Sandy Patty said, **" I am am so happy because"** and she started to sing " **His eye is on the sparrow…. And I know, He is watching (over) me."** What timing. This was the grand sign, the ultimate fleece as this was **the very special "song" between me and my Creator and my best Friend. The very words that GOD had used only a few times before to confirm any major issue or change**. GOD's sign for me that HIS plan was for me to marry Patricia. I finished my email in seconds with tears of joy running down my face, it read….

This is the email I sent to Patricia after I received my confirmation. *"I am possessed and fulfilled by your love. It is my night not to sleep but I am enjoying just lying in bed thinking of you, thinking of the day when you will be here with me, for the rest (interesting word "rest") of our lives.*

Written for January 21,2012.
Today, is our wedding day, we fulfill GOD's promise and receive HIS gift and start our new adventure in pursuit of what good things GOD has prepared for us to do."

…And they lived, **Happily ever after!**

92. The HAWK in 2011

While Patricia and I were still dating, I was driving down to Abbotsford to see her and I pulled off the road about halfway there on a logging road to sit for awhile by a river. As I drove down the logging road a hawk came and flew with me. It was unbelievable and I wish I had a camera.

The Hawk was just inches off the hood of my car and just in front of my window. He flew with me for about 300 yards.

This was another awesome sign. In my life when I was questioning my direction, GOD would send a bird, normally an Elijah (my favourite Bible character) type Raven or Crow to fly in front of me to show I am going in the right direction.

This hawk was far more beautiful than any old crow but then so is my Bride- to-be.

93: GOD TOLD ME I was RUDE !

GOD woke me up at 3:00am to say:

GOD said: *" You're Rude ! "*
I replied: "Excuse me, I don't think I am rude."
GOD: "*You never say please"*
Me: " I do too, I almost always try and be polite to people"
GOD: *" Not to me."*

And HE left me to ponder.

Let me think of some things I say in words to GOD or in prayer:

" Lord, bless this person"
" Bless this food"
" I ask that you heal ....."
" Give us a safe trip"
" Protect...
" Help ...

I understand. True, when I have been asking or praying to GOD, I speak as a command or order and not with a "Please Attitude".

HAVE A Grateful heart

94: Lloyd's wife HELEN, can you forgive others.

Helen was my brother Lloyds wife. I do not know Helen's story very well but I will tell which is all from my point of view.

Helen, after the divorce in 1968 (or so) was pretty much rejected and disowned by my family. This is totally normal in a divorce; each side takes a side and defends their own not only by showing their support but by their rejection and maybe even demonizing the other.

I have decided to take the concept that Lloyd talked about in his earlier letter, not to take sides but to love both no matter what. This has been seen by society and many friends as not only just strange but very wrong. I refer you back to I Corinthians 13 and the Lord's prayer where we are instructed to forgive others and love each other.
   As I have said or will say again is the Lord's prayer seems to me to be backwards but I believe was said that way to deliberately enforce the issue.

" forgive us our sins as we forgive others," and then Christ goes on in a few verses later to really hit it home in case you missed it. If you don't forgive others, then His Father (GOD) who is in heaven will not forgive you." Ouch.. Major ouch… eternal ouch.

This is important…..

Back to Helen. After my wife Gwen died in 2010 and I was getting married to Patricia in 2012 we were doing up the wedding invitations and I thought a serious wrong needed to be righted. I must find Helen and invite her. As I stated in the above story of Lloyd, Lloyd was more like a father to me and along that same line, Helen played an important part like my Mother. My Mother had passed away in 1996 and I wanted Helen to be my very special guest at the wedding.

I knew this would cause problems within my family, especially with my older brothers who were closer to Lloyd than me. Some of them had not spoken to Helen, I believe, since the divorce which was about 44 years. I did get some push back from my brothers when I let them know she was invited.

They told me they did not think it was a good idea, I told them she was invited and coming as my very special guest and that all my brothers were invited too. If Helen's coming offended them, they should first read their Bible and second maybe learn the real facts and not put the blame of the divorce and Lloyds demise all on her.

It worked out and some reconciliation happened.

I write this story because so often miss information, belief, culture or just life creates conflicts. I return to what I think are two critical factors of living.

1) FORGIVE, no matter what. You read " Can you forgive a pedophile" which I felt took forgiving to the the limit.

2) LOVE ONE ANOTHER, as Lloyd said, or more import, as Christ said was the new commandment and that is how you will know that you are a follower of Christ.

No matter what !

Dimes became a very important part of my life just before Gwen died. One day, we were sorting the closest, she liked to do that, she was organizing things to give away to her friends, many who could not afford such beautiful things. We opened one drawer and there was dime, I thought nothing of it.

Gwen sat down on the floor and cried. I asked her what was it. She said, for years, she would find dimes in the most unusual places and she believe that it was her Mom, just letting her know she was watching over her, assuring her that everything would be alright.

Then she said, when I get to heaven, I will try and send you dimes when you need comfort, assurance or confirmation. I don't know if they will be from me or from GOD, but I will ask if we can do that. She gave me that dime.

Judge for yourself and come up with your own conclusion.

1) 2010 the Christmas Dime story. It has it's own chapter. Likely the most amazing of them all.

2) 2010   Just had lunch with Kim and we chatted about how each other was doing after Gwen's death. When I returned to my car, there by my door on the ground was a dime. I showed Kim. 2006 dime.

3) 2011 Feb. I had walked the whole of our acres seeking a place where we were to build the what was then the Stewardship Center and we now call"**The Rock**". GOD had said where I find the dime I was to do it. I searched the whole property and found nothing. Tired and discouraged I came home and got a cup of coffee and sat down in my favorite chair in the Living room of the house. I leaned forward to pray and there between my feet on the carpet was a dime. A USA dime, it says, "In God we trust".

   3) 2011 March Went golfing with my good friend Pastor Harry. My son and company were going to Seattle for a business trip so we hopped on board the private jet and went and

played a great game of golf on Freddy Couple's special coarse.

Not planned that way, but ended up there. Like so many other times, the day was Ok but looked like it might get really ugly. Coming up the 18th fairway a few guys in front let us thru. We hurried 18 as a storm was coming and then ran after our putts to the club house.

We just made it to the big covered archway entrance for cars was when a fierce wind and thunder storm rain pelted down. We were dry, but just by a hair. Later we caught the plane home and what a take off, I am sure that plane was at a 45 degree angle sideways. The pilot dropped us off in Victoria where we were going to golf with another buddy, Steve, for few days. We played there and then made it to the club house for lunch.

Funny note, that pilot who we used many times ended up at Christmas dinner table the first year I knew Patricia at her family's house. He is related to her. Back to the story...

We sat in a chair in the golf club house and some of the old boys came by and said it was their table, I was going to say something rude but we just moved on. Then the waiter asked us to move as they were not serving that area, so we moved again. I put my thing down and went to the bathroom, when I came back, a friend of Steves had sat where I had put my stuff. Now I was still suffering from depression and mourning as had not recovered from my wife's death yet. That April 1 letter of "though I walk thru the valley of the shadow of death would be written in about a week, so that was my mental state. There were no other chairs at the table so I grabbed one from another table and move it over. I sat down, put my stuff under my seat and after all that shuffling, there was dime, under that chair. I am with you Deryl, just stay calm and enjoy your friends and golf.

5) 2011 I was cleaning out the Chute Lake house after the sale and moving on with my life. After Gwen's death in Sept 2010, going back to the house was hard, so many memories. I was cleaning out that drawer where Gwen had found the original dime, and there was another one.

6) 2011 I was visiting a client, a young man with a young family, his Dad had died sometime ago and was wondering if I should quit my job. By my door of the car was a dime. 1989. I picked it up and GOD said, Be the Father to many. Don't quit your job, you have done this for over 40 years and your experience is needed to help others. I didn't give you 40 years of training in your work to just have you throw it away to do just " ministry"**, it is all ministry.**

7) 2011   Oct. Patricia was moving into my condo and moving to Kelowna so we could date. When I opened the front door there was a very bright light almost blinding coming off the middle of the black marble floor.   I covered my eyes and went to see what it was. It was a dime, reflecting the light off the above ceiling pot light. GOD's blessing on us. I had scrubbed that place clean the day before for my girl, and no one else had keys.

8) 2011 Nov. Went to pick up the return labels which Patricia had order to put on all our wedding invitations. I pulled my wallet out to pay and a dime struck to my glasses and stuck there. I shook it off and it fell right into the middle of the Deryl & Patricia new return address labels. God was blessing our marriage.

9) 2012 Feb. I was at the bank to sign a big mortgage on my condo so I could do a few thing I needed to do up at The Rock. I did not want to get into debt again but with rates so low, seemed the best option. Just before I signed the mortgage papers in the guys office I looked under my chair and there was a dime. Go ahead Deryl, it is the right thing to do.

10) 2012 Nov. We had just finished building the Train Shed, a big expense for just model trains, but it would be a place the grandkids and I would play once and even twice every week. I remember my grandson Taylen told his Dad once when I was away on vacation, "I am getting Train Shed withdrawal, when is Grampa back ?" very special place it turned out to be.   But then we had just finished it and I was standing by the doorway in the November mud. I asked GOD, was this a wise use of that money?   I looked down and there between my feet in the mud was a dime. 2006.

11) 2012 Dec. Was on vacation stuck at an airport. I had bought a book on Stock Reviews for 2013 and I was planning my 2013 business stuff wondering again if I should just retire. When I went to pay for the book a dime was stuck to my VISA card and I had a hard time getting it off. It was a 2013 dime. Yes, carry on, you are on the right path.

12) 2013 March. I was walking in the snow down a forested path with my 4 best buds, The Platoon, the leaders of Men of KGF and we were just to start our first men's weekend camp retreat. On the path in the middle of nowhere was a dime. Keep it up boys, good job.

13) 2013 May We were in Europe in Verimoitta, Italy. Enjoying the sites when a wedding car parade came beeping their horns and the whole town stopped, came out to the stores and cheered. There must have been 20 cars and more joined in, all decorated up. The whole community rejoiced. As I stood there thinking this is how life should be with us rejoicing together like that, either at a wedding, a birth or even at a funeral. That is what The Rock, our place needs to be like. I looked down and between my feet was coin but not a silvery dime, it was copper, but an old coin, a 10 Krona.

14) 2013 June. The men's ministry at the church was going well. We had two very good weekend retreats as well as other events. But as usual, one day I was a little down as I was getting no reply from the guys on something I had asked. I wondered outside after Sunday service and Benita, my good friend Rolly's wife stopped her car and rolled her window down to talk to me. Just wanted to thank me for the great job I was doing with the men and she told me a story of how it impacted someone close to her in a good way. She drove away and under the wheels of her car were 2 dimes. My first double dime.... Both 2010, I started to attend that church in Nov 2010

15) 2013 June I was trying to decide what the focus would be at our next Gardom lake Weekend Men's retreat. Details next story.

16) 2013 June. Amazing stories that also have their own chapter, My fleece to leave KGF Church and help Monty start up EPIC City Church. 2 dimes, same year, both the year of Pastor Monty's birth.

17) 2013 July confirming dime for EPIC, see full story in its own chapter.

18) 2013 July.   Again questioning going to EPIC and leaving the Men's ministry at KGF Church, in my coffee holder was a 1994 dime. The year representing the start of a great ministry.

19) 2013 Sept, found in Starbucks. Was worried about the new Men's Ministry I was starting, I was meeting the guys at Starbucks to plan it. A 1994 dime. 1994 was when I moved back to Comox and wanted to start a Men's Ministry, rather God had me do the Cumberland Boys Club, which turned out to be the best Men's Ministry I ever did as about 12 of us guys worked with the boys.

20) Oct 2013   found two dimes in a very strange way, didn't write down so can't remember where expect I have asked many times what they could be, I know they are important.   1961 & 2007. 2007 I know, great prosperity and opportunity, but don't now the 1961, still waiting.

21) Oct 2013   We were just leaving KGF church, I did my last men's meeting and was heading home, very discouraged. I did not want to give up leading the Men of KGF as I loved it but knew I was to move onto EPIC City Church.   I stopped at the gas station where I first found that dime when I was going for coffee with Monty that told me I was to leave. I went in and the girl behind the counter struggled with my change. She gave me most but two dimes dropped to the floor and rolled away. I found them, a 1996 and 2010.   1996 was the end of my wonderful run of the Cumberland Boys Club ministry and 2010 was the end of my almost 40 year marriage to Gwen. Both were ends, but both were new starts. The question was, what I would do with it.

22) 2013 Nov. Lost my largest Kamloops client who was a good friend as well I lost my office space as all my partners jumped ship and were going to let a bank take over that office. I was not going back there. I was feeling lost and disappointed. I found two dimes. 1978 and 2007. We actually got our transfer notice to Comox for the awesome new start in late Dec 1978 and moved early Jan 1979. 2007 is the year my business took off to the moon and became totally self sustaining. Moved to 2nd in all of Canada of 600 in the company in just 5 years. 1st had been around for over 10 years.

23) 2014 jan. We were in Vegas for New Years. Awesome. I told Patricia, I am Vegas, I am going to check and see if I can find a dime under a slot machine and if I do, I will play it. This is not likely GOD's intent on the dimes to confirm. I looked at over a 100 chairs and table, nothing, I said, well, it does not surprise me, maybe GOD is not here in Vegas. We were heading to our room and decided to just stop at the front desk to see if there was a quick way to check out in the morning. They likely had a dozen or more clerks, we were at the Parisenne, finally a clerk opened up and when we asked about a quick exit our of hotel and Vegas, I looked down and by my foot was a 2004 dime. The overall marble floor was spotless everywhere, how they missed that, I don't know, and who used a dime to pay a hotel bill in Vegas.

24) 2014 Feb. Was meeting my best friend for coffee to discuss EPIC City Church stuff. At the door I found two dimes. 1968 and 2011. I told him, I understand the 2011, that is when you and I first meet to do Men of KGF but I have no idea about the 1968 ? He said that was his birth year.

25) 2014 April took my love Patricia golfing for the first time, nervous about it. Paid for our drinks and the clerk dropped a dime on the floor. He picked it up and said, this must be your lucky dime and lucky day. It was a 2012, the year Patricia and I were married.

26) 2014 March. Beautiful day on the beach with my Grandkids at Disney World. My eldest grandson was digging a big hole in the sand and down deep he found a funny coin. It looked like a big copper penny, but it was a 10 Centavos. That grandson and I share the same middle name.

27) 2014 march Found a dime in the Garden Railway at Disney World. This fall, I am starting a new Senior men's ministry every Weds morning, we are going to build a Garden Railway up here at The Rock.

28) 2014 July. Patricia was driving to Vancouver over the Coquahalla Hyway, a high mountain pass and I was nervous. I looked at her old car and said, no, you are not going over there in that so I bought her a new Jeep. My son mentioned a good friend of his had her car just breakdown and she could not afford to repair it much less buy a used one. We decided to give her Patricia's Toyota, it still ran well and was good for going to and from work in town for my son's friend. When she came and picked up the car, when she was looking it over, we found a dime under the car. Our blessing for gifting her the car, well done.

29) 2014 Nov. I was preparing to do a sermon at our church. It was the Cumberland Boys club story, then the Gibson's porn or God story and finished with the forgiving story of killing the pedophile. I was very nervous as they are not something I wanted to say in public. I was driving and discussing it with GOD, telling I thought maybe it was a little too ugly of a message for a Sunday morning church service, maybe just good for one on one with another man. HE said; go to the gas station where you got that Christmas dime. I did. Bought what I bought back then and got two dimes. I could hardly wait to see the years, a 1979 and 2002. Wow. 1979 I was moved to Comox from Prince George, after much struggling, a new and great start. 2002 was when the year I left banking and started my own business. Both the start of new, exciting and very rewarding new era. If I had not given that talk back then in public, granted to friends, I would have never had the nerve to publish this book, as is.

30) 2015 July. We were having a planning meeting for the fall and trying to decide what subject, focus or series we would do. I told the guys I had found a 2001 dime on the pool deck outside and had no idea what it meant. Rob nudged me and said, look at the bottom of the screen of this DVD series we were considering, it said, " 2001 copyright". We did it, it was very good.

2016 Nov   Was in Merritt and was to give a talk to the Men's breakfast there. I was going to do the Cumberland Boys club story again and follow with the Gibson story of choosing porn over GOD. Woke up that morning very nervous, found a dime on the floor by my bed. I got to the fireside room at the church early to get a feel of the place. The tables were all set so I found a spot and put my coat on the chair. I was not comfortable with that so decided to move and moved to the other side and put my coat on that chair. I moved the chair to sit down and there was a dime on the floor under that last chair.   Acknowledgment to carry on.

31) There are numerous more dime stories but I didn't always write it down in my journal right away. I figured, oh yeah, I will remember that one, but I can't.

Good to keep a journal so you can see what GOD has done.

96. Porn magazine in Church waiting table. In 2012

Got your attention on that one didn't I. Well there was.

I was sitting in my church's waiting room as I had a meeting with the pastor and I was early. I wanted to talk to him about an idea I had on running a porn session for the men of the church. Of course we label it as a "Purity Session" or something as porn is more or less a taboo word in most church circles.

I was nervous and getting second thoughts. I told GOD that I really didn't want to get back into the sewer again and deal with the porn issue. I said I would like to get on the positive side and discuss **"Being the man God made me to be !"** GOD said men can't be that men until they clean up their act (not HIS exact words). I asked for a sign.

"OK" GOD said, *"how about there is a naked woman on the back of that magazine beside you, if there is, will you do what I am asking and do the porn sessions?"* I figured I had GOD on this one. I was in a Mennonite church sitting in the pastors waiting room and the magazine GOD was talking about was the Mennonite Brethren Herald. **No way HE was winning this bet.**

I picked it up and held it. GOD said, *"Come on, turn it over, what is the matter, are you afraid ?"* Sometimes GOD's sense of humour is a little too much for me. I was afraid, I was very afraid and strongly believed that there **would not** be that picture on the back and that magazine and all this talk of GOD was just my wild imagination.

Anyways, it took some time and I finally turned it over. On the back page was a full page colour picture of Adam and Eve, naked except for appropriately placed wording, "Honouring GOD with the Body, A study on Human Sexuality. " I took the magazine for my proof that GOD was speaking to me and have it my spiritual binder.

We did the series.

97: Gardom Lake Men's retreat dime story , Summer 2013

We had a great men's retreat weekend in the spring and were planning another in fall. Problem though, many guys had told me they really loved the retreat and wanted to bring their sons the next time. The other guys said "no" they didn't want any kids there.

What to do.

"So GOD", I asked, "what do we do... Father and Sons weekend or just Men's weekend." I was working out the pros and cons of both in my head while at the same time helping my Grandson with his school project to build a "model of Fort Victoria". I was very confused and couldn't decide, do it one way and half the guys said they wouldn't come, do it the other way and the other half won't come.

My Grandson said he just needed a pinch more of sawdust. We were gluing sawdust to the model as dried grass. Problem was, the week before he had used up all the sawdust and what was left, I had vacuumed up. I said I didn't have any more, but wait, there was just a pinch under the back foot of the saw. I reached behind the saw bench and picked it up, it was a little crusty. In the pinch of sawdust was a dime.

I picked up the dime. It was an older dime, the same year as my eldest son's birth year. OK, I told the guys, we are doing the Father and Son weekend in the fall at Gardom Lake Bible Camp.

The guys who had said they did not want a Father & Son camp said they would bring a boy who didn't have a Father to take him and would bring him along. Great idea.

We had a full camp and an AMAZING life changing weekend and my eldest son joined me and we did a session together...

That was likely the best part.

99: ONE DAY! I WILL RULE A WORLD ! in 2013

My BAND OF BROTHERS, the tribe of five. My heart aches and rejoices over these thoughts, what could have been and what was. In all my years of serving GOD I never had a greater Band of Brothers as great as these.

I think it was 2012 and I was ready to get back to church and start the Men's Ministry my heart had always desired. Patricia and I had started to attend KGF (Kelowna Gospel Fellowship church in Kelowna) and I was asking around about who would be interested in starting a men's ministry. The name "Troy" kept coming up and apparently you need to talk to "Deryl" was told to him. Finally one Sunday we met and a great spiritual adventure would begin.

We needed to form a leadership team. Troy asked if he could bring his friend Colin, yes. Pastor Mike introduced me to Monty, he was using that church as his starting point as he was on a path to plant a new church. Monty asked if he could bring his friend Jim, and the "five" were established.

We met every Friday morning before work in the church Fireside room. The depth of those meetings could never be repeated, the soul searching, the honesty, the relationships. The timing was perfect.

We did two Gardom Bible Camp men's retreats of which are detailed in other stories.

I cannot get into the details as it would break confidentiality, but if you can ever get into a group that have removed all their masks, **DO IT**. It was beyond awesome. But … we are in a spiritual war and the enemy did his work. One by one we lost a brother, I regret we could not have reached out to each as they left and still loved them, but time and whatever slowly got between us and until we had all gone our separate ways.

I think too we lost our way when we moved out of the private Fireside room in the church and started to meet at Starbucks.

But much good was done. **It was the right time for each of our needs, for each season in our journey there is a reason.** Lives were transformed and now each of us has a separate ministry.

Anyway, the story that changed everything: I think we were at Gardom Lake. The five of us had gone up early to prepare and were walking in the woods. I was talking about how when I get to heaven, I understand we will be ruling worlds with Christ.

I stated that I knew I was nowhere close to be given such responsibility because if I was the ruler of a world, I would not allow such greed that more money would be spent on war than on feeding the poor, I would nuke idiots that cut me off when driving and I would obliterate all pedophiles from the face of eternity.

Then Troy said to me; " **what if, when GOD asks you to go and rule over a world, that HE asks the same HE asked HIS son Jesus who is to rule over this earth, but rather than to rule over them, to die for them and their sins ... first ...**"

I was speechless and tears overwhelmed me.

100. GOD attacked me in a rage..

I had a most vivid dream one night.

I was talking to the Holy Spirit and HE was trying to talk to me about something but I was not paying much attention. Also I did not like what HE was suggesting and I was telling HIM my opinion which I thought was a much better idea.

(Where have we heard that before…OK, you might think by now I am crazy for arguing with GOD, but remember Moses did and actually changed GOD's mind at the time. GOD wanted to just wipe the Israelites out and Moses talked HIM into giving them another chance. Also, you may not believe you argue or disagree with GOD, but if you are not doing HIS will, then you have ignored HIM and just did your own thing. Back to the story…)

With that ALMIGHTY GOD THE FATHER appeared.
HE was enormous in size, flowing robe and HE was very angry.
Angry at me. In a thunder HE rushed towards me in fury yelling:

Who do you think you are ?
Did you make the heavens and the earth ?
The things I have seen you build on your own have all blow up in your face. You did not create the success of the Cumberland Boys Club, I did ! You did not have the great success in Bank, you destroyed it ! Any time you have tried to stand on your own, you have failed, miserably !

Now we have come to you with the privilege to do something with US. And you treat US with contempt !!!
You are so full of pride, greed and self .
Tell me oh wise Deryl,
Why should I not just strike you dead where you stand ?
What gives you right to stand in front of ME, ALMIGHTY GOD ?

At that point, the very GOD of the Old Testament was just inches from my face and HIS whole Holy and Just countenance overwhelming me and about to bring all the wrath I deserved upon me and I was literally scared to death, when ……….

In a flash, at the last moment, Jesus jumped between us with HIS arms stretched out wide to block GOD's wrath, and said.

"I do. I paid the price, I have made Deryl Holy, Righteous, Pure, Forgiven and your Beloved Son ."

GOD sees me thru the blood stained rose coloured glasses of Christ.

Sometimes I think we hear and believe too much in the 'love" of GOD. HE is, but most of all HE is Holy. He is also just.

We are told that the FEAR of GOD is the beginning of wisdom. Especially me, I have to remember my place when I come boldy before the throne.

101….GOD helped me in CALLING CARDS & GOLF .

I spent most of the evenings after Gwen's death at the casino. From November to March, after work I would wander down there and sat at the Black Jack table then head home about 11:00 pm so that I would just fall asleep and not be home alone at night.

I started with $100.00 and it lasted me the whole time. Actually, I managed to grow it to my all time high of just over 600.00 by March 28. My secret was, GOD would call cards for me once in awhile. I never told anyone this as calling the cards was weird enough and almost got me kicked out.

I would never know when, but then GOD would say, go ahead and call the next card out loud before dealt, it will be a 5 of hearts or whatever, 5 of hearts was my favorite call. I would get the go ahead on that when I had been dealt a 16 already, the worst hand in blackjack and the 5 would give me a 21, a win or at worst, a push. (a push is a tie)

I guess GOD knew I was hurting and that HE could not get me out of the casino as I felt safe there so HE just protected me. I never won too big and never lost my original amount until the last days of March. I lost it all on March 30 & March 31 and walked away. You see, on April 1 the golf course was opening and I was moving my time from the casino to the golf course.

Effective April 1, I was on the course all my awaking hours and in the club house in with the guys till late. I remember once I was talking with the Pro and a guy asked, "do you either of you work here ? " The Pro said, "I work here, but he, (refer to me,) lives here." We all laughed.

For most of the time, I just wandered the holes, kept focused on the game not on my life. I met about five other men my age doing the same thing and all of them had lost their wives that winter too.

My game improved, I went from an 18 handicap to a Scratch. That means shooting on a good day from 90 a round to 72. I played over 150 rounds from April 1 to Aug 1 and I won the B side of the club championship, the A side was the Pro's. I also got to play in the lead group in the charity tourney with Dave Barr and Blake Como.
   I had achieved my all my golfing goals.

On my birthday in late July, a hot summer's day in the Okanagan of BC, I turned 60 and I walked and carried my clubs for 60 holes. My favorite number is the number 8, as I am the 8th son. 60 holes is just over 3 rounds, I shot 88 on my first round, 88 on 2nd and on the third drained a 30 foot put to score ... 88. The old man didn't lose any momentum. Black Mountain course is a very hilly course with much elevation change and I don't think anyone had ever walked it before, much less 60 holes.

The day after the tournament, I went out and shot 104, unbelievable, but I had lost my drive, my desire and could not focus on the game anymore. Soon after I meet Patricia and pretty much did not play golf except an odd time for the next five years. That was OK as I had found a better life.

The golf, walking in the fresh air, the talks with GOD, was good therapy.

102: GOD gave me one last game of Black Jack. In 2015

We were on a cruise ship where I enjoyed playing a late night at the Blackjack table after dinner and show of formal night. I used to go in my tux feeling like James, James Bond.

But GOD stopped by to chat, He said*:" now that you are working with guys with various addictions and I know you don't have a problem with gambling but you should consider giving it up if you are serious about helping others with their addictions. "*
I thought about it... ummmmmmmmmmmm ????

HE continued by sweetening the pot*: "if you agree to quit, I will give you the most exciting game of your life. I know how you love to call cards, so go ahead, the first hand you will get will be 16, (the worst hand in Blackjack,) but do as you love to do and call out loud for the 5, even make it the 5 of hearts. You will get it and much more to come. Enjoy."*

So, we had a great supper and then watched the show all dressed up. We headed for the casino with my allocated $100.00. I found what looked like a friendly and talkative table and sat down. My first card was a 10 followed by, yup, a 6. Oh yeah, as the dealer got a 10. I said loudly so all could hear, "Give me a 5 of hearts". I got it, 21... yehaaa, off to great start. The dealer got blackjack and I lost that hand. I gasped in shock.

Next hand I got an Ace, was very excited, especially when the next card was another Ace, and the dealer got 10 again... Perfect, split and double the money. I got two 10's which gave me two black jacks. Wow, so pumped. The dealer got backjack again and I lost my doubled down bet. I said I got Blackjack, but she said I didn't get it my 1st 2 cards like she did. OUCH !

I did recover and was up from original $100.00 to $150.00 and like a good boy, pocketed my original $100.00. But of course, after losing $40.00 of the winnings I got a perfect double down on my last $10.00, but then to double down I would need to dip back into my pocket from my original $100.00. I did and it went south very fast from there.

AN EPIC JOURNEY
103 . EPIC dime story. in June 2013

"Only if I hear DIRECTLY from GOD Himself will I be going with you to EPIC. My last instruction from GOD was to serve at KGF church so unless I hear otherwise, I am staying at KGF"
Pretty much my first words to my now buddy and Pastor Monty when we met back in Oct 2012.

In May of 2013 the thought of helping out at the church plant called EPIC City Church was starting to pre-occupy my thoughts. So I had a chat with GOD and said "OK look, I have to stop thinking about going to EPIC and focus on what we are going to do with the Men at KGF Church in the fall. So, **I am going to put out a fleece**, and if I get the fleece, I will go help Monty at Epic, if I don't, then this is the last I will think of it and focus on Men of KGF.

In that You (GOD) seem to like using the dimes with me lately to affirm things, here is the deal, **if I find a dime one day in an obscure place when I am going to meet with Monty and the dime has his birth year on it,** I will help Monty with the church plant of EPIC City Church." I had no idea how old he was. I was on a train in Italy at the time.

When I got home, I was heading to our normal 6:00 am coffee/accountability meeting with the guys. Troy texted us while I was enroute saying he was in Vancouver and would not make it. That was followed by the others texting they would not make it either because of various reasons. Oh man, I had dragged my butt out of bed at 5:30 am and was on the road already to meet and looking like I would be alone. Then I got a text from Monty saying he could make it, but wouldn't be available till 7:00 am and could we meet out his way at Starbucks in Glenmore.

"Sure" I texted back.

I had some time to blow and was just passing the gas station at KLO and Benvoulin so decided to get a coffee. I remember there were 6 parking stalls available and I was heading for the one closest to the door and then decided to veer off and take a different one. I was not that old, I could walk.

I got out of my car and there **on the parking lot pavement right by my door was an old dime.** Um... what year, **I noted the year.** Um.... I wonder what year Monty was born ? I had no idea.

When I got to have coffee with Monty I didn't say anything about the dime for a long time, then I finally asked him, "what year were you born ?" He said, **"such and such a year". Wow.... the fleece was totally filled to the letter, that was the same year as on the dime.** I stood up and shook Monty's hand saying " Well, if you will have me, it looks like **I am coming to EPIC ! "**

And I am loving it, a great place to worship with those who are now some of my closest friends.

98: A SHOOTING STAR at GARDOM in 2015

We were having an EPIC City Church family camp at Gardom Lake Bible Retreat and Bible camp up in the woods. It was a great camp with the only purpose was to build relationships. No speakers, no agenda, just hang out around the old stove, walking in the wood, swimming or canoeing in the lake, playing some board games together or shooting hoops in the gym.

The first night, I had told everyone we would have a camp fire at 9:00 pm, if they had a guitar to bring it along and we could do some campfire songs. I got the staff to get the fire going but no one came. I was so disappointed, it was like the day after again in Grade 1 when no one came. I had visualized this beautiful camp fire family night, not only with my church family but my whole family and grandkids were there too. But no one was at the campfire. I went looking but didn't really find anyone. Where were they?

I stopped halfway back between the campfire and the lodge and it was pitch black way out in those woods. The occasional owl would call but other than that, quiet. I came to an opening in the trees and I could see the sky filled with stars. I looked up with tears coming down my face and asked GOD, where is everyone, are they bored, am I the only one having a beautiful weekend just being there with them and YOU ?

Looking at the heavens and opening my arms out wide like I was saying, why??? Then the most beautiful, fullest shooting star went all the way across the night sky in front of me and then it was gone.

I heard the campfire, a guitar, some laughter and chatter. I made it back to the campfire and there they were, all gathered around having a beautiful time together, wondering where I was.

Talking with GOD I said, just talking to GOD.

104: The Rock" Dime # 27 story.
First ever double dime triple header.

Monty called in sick so it was just one buddy and I for Weds AM coffee. I was going to cancel as I hate getting up before 6:00am just for coffee at Starbucks, but went anyway. We both agreed that meeting for the sake of meeting was not what we wanted, we wanted a challenge, a pursuit, a purpose. Also, **we have great things we have been called to do,** the first being our new church start called Epic City Church and then what we are going to at "The Rock" (my place). We agreed that we don't want to be sitting here in another year from now just having coffee and still talking about what we "should do", **we want to do.**

We got into a great discussion around focusing on **helping others going from good to great and great to awesome.** That sitting talking about our own problems, issues or even dreams as an accountability partners would not get us much further. The best thing in order **to be the person we want to be and that GOD made us to be is to start helping others. Never seen anyone really grow by just talking about themselves. You can heal talking about your issues but not grow. You need to help others to grow.**

So what then. Interesting that our church is in the Martin Centre, which is the home for the boys and girls club. Talking about making people better we thought to look at Jesus's example. **He took 12 men and changed the world.** The ideal for serving others. My buddy mentioned that they figure that 11 of the 12 disciples of Jesus were just boys. We'll, under age anyway. John was likely only 16. I have no idea if this is true but He had lots to back up his claim.

So what can we do... Bring guys together, maybe Father/son, maybe family. Working and playing together with purpose. This could include things like hockey on the rink, floor hockey in the summer and capture the flag up at the rock, followed by a camp fire chat. Or better yet, could include **having others to help build it.** Who wouldn't want to drive a tractor or bobcat and move some dirt ?

I left the coffee shop very excited and challenged. For years now, I believe GOD has been affirming things for me with dimes. I have 26 stories already. As I left, **I found two dimes,** a 1968 and a 2011. I understood the 2011, as that was my year of new starts and getting things going again after many years as a caregiver and my wife dying of cancer in late 2010. In 2011, I restarted my business, achieved my life goal at golf became a scratch golfer and won a tournament, sailed the Desolation Sound with two buds, which we had discussed doing for 20 years, and meet and proposed to my wonderful bride Patricia who I had not seen for 40 years.

The 1968 dime, what was that about ? I texted my buddy who I just had the great chat with and asked what year was he born. 1968 he texted back, why? I said we just got confirmation. How often do you see an old dime, especially that old, heck, as old as him.

I got in my car and had to drive just 1 minute to my next place and had the radio on. All that I had time to hear on the radio on this short trip was this: " today's moment in time is **focused on 1968**, a speech from then Prime Minister Lester Pearson who said " **the decisions and action we are taking today will have a major impact on the young men and women and generations to come** ." Or something like that, I was at my next stop. Wow, how appropriate and how crazy that I would be in the car for only that length of time and then to talk about that year and that same topic My buddy and I had agreed to commit to, and as he would say, not just any shake but a covenant shake grasping each other's wrists. Boh-yah...

Well, my brain was flying and I could not focus at work so decided to go home to The Rock to take some quiet time and listen to what GOD was saying. I have heard many times that we need do take the time to just listen. I went home and sat in the hot tub with the sun shining down but about minus 15 degrees. Ok GOD talk I am listening.

As Patricia and I sat in the hot tub, I noticed a half a dozen Quail had cuddled up by the hot tub seeking refuge and safety from the cold. All of sudden there was a great noise and flapping of wings right beside us. A hawk had dove trying I assume to catch one of the Quail. He was followed by a second hawk. Sitting in the tub and have the Quail screaming and fleeing for safety of the deck and the hawks screeching after them.

All was over in seconds and all were safe, though I am sure all of our hearts were pounding. **That was what we were looking at doing, protecting other for the enemies attacks, especially our young.**

No word yet, so decided to walk the garbage cans down the .4 km driveway to the road. I normally take the tractor down but it has a flat tire and dead battery, likely both from the cold. The walk was gorgeous on this winter day overlooking the winter wonderland view of the Okanagan valley below. On my way back, halfway up I heard GOD speak to my soul. He said*: "Yes, I like to do things in threes when they are important. You got the dime and two of the three 1968's and you already know the third".* I said: GOD, I have no clue what the third is. How about some help, that is why I came to listen. He said*: "where was I in 1968 when we started this conversation and HE made me a promised."*

I was overwhelmed as I remembered the moment back in 1968 when I was just a teen, as if it was happening right then. I was junior counselor at Hope Bay Bible Camp on Pender Island. The summer was spent with me in charge of the sports. I had found this big old tree in the forest as my Holy Place where I would go to be quiet and talk to GOD and listen. GOD told me at the time, you see this, referring to the camp where Christians came to play games, sports and spend good times together and grow spiritually. One day, you will have a place like this.

"The Rock" is the fulfillment of that promise almost 50 years ago, *but the timing with so many other things is PERFECT.*

105 . To STAY or to GO ? March 2016

I was at a crossroads in life and a choice was needed. Do I continue to attend and participate at the church I was going to or do I move on to newer adventures ?

Going to church had lost its desire. I didn't feel I was serving or if serving I was definitely doing it wrong. I didn't feel I was going to worship GOD but rather to deal with issues and people. Confront people rather than loving/caring for them. Was I doing more harm than good? Was it time to move on, had I done what GOD had asked me to do when HE asked me to go and support (Pastor) Monty at this new church plant?

Maybe I am just a starter and after two years create more grief.

In my past life as a Bank Manager, we moved pretty much every two years. I would come in, get the branch running well, then leave. I did that 18 times before I left the banks. I have been just over two years at EPIC City Church, maybe it was time for the next project.

So I asked GOD, "what do you want???" Is it time for me to move on or stay? Please let me know. GOD was very precise on me coming to EPIC, but had not said anything about it now for almost three years. "I need clarification Lord."

I started to find fault with most things and most people. Frustration overtook serving. Exhaustion overtook enthusiasm.

I repeatedly asked GOD for an answer, a sign, any indication, an exit door, permission to leave. I begged, pleaded and prayed, but HE was silent. One day, just before Easter I climbed to the top of our summit and cried out for direction. Nothing. Nothing but silence. This is not unusual, as GOD usually does things in HIS own way and time. HE is likely seeing if I am really sincere and to see if I will just take matters into my own hands.

Then the other morning, I had finished breakfast and devotions and was just sitting in my chair, trying to think of nothing and GOD replied. HE replied in HIS usual brief and to the point manner that I am accustomed to, as this was not a relationship building moment. It was GOD Almighty, giving HIS command. The hair on the back of my neck stood on end and my eyes filled with tears, as seems to happen when GOD draws near.

A picture or vision came into my head, of which I was very familiar with only mine was the same place thousands of years ago.

It was the Port of Joppa (Jaffa) in Isreal. I was there in 2015 and the key is a large statue of a Great Fish between the buildings by the port. Jonah's Great Fish as this is where Jonah fled from GOD after GOD had told him to go to Ninivah, and Jonah ran away instead.

Then God said, " *I told you to go and support (Pastor) Monty at EPIC (City Church), I have not instructed you otherwise. Are you going to obey or run away?* "

Do you find that too, God usually doesn't give you a straight answer, but gives you a choice to choose. Accept HIM or reject HiM and follow your own path.

I will go back to EPIC with a passion to serve with all my heart.

A few days later, GOD returned to ask, " *I was wondering if you were going to love the people of EPIC like Jonah cared for the people of Ninivah, or are you going to love my children at EPIC like I love them ?* "

That was March and we continued to serve at EPIC until May 6, 2016 when GOD spoke to me that morning, " *It is time to build The Rock.*" *7:00 am, May 6, 2016.*

When chaos seems everywhere, look up, GOD is likely trying to get your attention.

I will go over a little history as this is a major event in our life and it was important to let our EPIC church family know why we were moving on.

106 . Letter to my Dear EPIC Family:

I know most of you found our announcement on Sunday that we are leaving EPIC and moving on to be very quick news and surprising. I would like to explain.

After my wife died in 2010, I was made caretaker of these 100 acres we are living on and asked if I wanted to move up onto the house on the property and be the caretaker. I agreed. When I arrived here I was wandering through the forest and ***GOD spoke to me saying HE was giving me this land to build something special for HIM***. He would let me know the details when the time was right.

Next, I reconnected for lunch with Patricia after not seeing her for over 40 years. We were having a nice lunch as two old friends catching up as I was avoiding women at the time and had NO intent on remarrying. I believed God had things for me to do and i didn't want any women getting in the way. Like Paul said about being single. Just minutes after we sat down for lunch at Earls on Top, ***God showed and said to me " This is my gift to you, she will be your Help-Mate, marry her ".*** I was scared, flabbergasted and totally taken off guard. As my son said, I spent the next two dates drilling her with a million questions on her spiritual beliefs; He said I was treating her more like a job interview than courting or dating. But I was making sure GOD was right with his pick. As you all know, GOD was absolutely right, Patricia was literally a "GOD send" for me. I asked her to marry me on our 5th date to the shock of everyone, including me. Yes, I have a history of moving fast **when GOD speaks.**

I was working on the concept of what "The Rock" should be and GOD would show me little glimpses of this and that but never gave me the go ahead to really start.

So how did I end up at EPIC City Church instead and working with Monty ? I first met Monty at KGF (Kelowna Gospel Fellowship) Church, both of us were new to KGF and he was to start the preliminary of EPIC and Pastor Mike introduced us and said we should work together. I was just starting up the Men of KGF.

After Mike left I told Monty that I knew God wanted me to start up the Men of KGF and that I WAS NOT GOING TO EPIC unless I heard from **GOD Himself.** Rather rude but I thought I should lay my cards on the table. Then to my absolute shock once again, after 1 year doing Men of KGF *God said, " Go support Monty in the start up of EPIC"*. I told the dime story to pastor Mike at KGF that GOD had called me to go to EPIC so I wrapped things up at KGF and moved onto EPIC . I put " The Rock" on hold to help Monty with EPIC until I heard from GOD otherwise.

I woke up Friday morning, May 6th and heard *God say, " It is time for The Rock"*. I was shocked. I knew Monty was working on the EPIC Vision and it would be discussed at a full church meeting in just over a week. If I was to make such a big move, I would need to let him know so he could adjust the EPIC Vision and planning accordingly. I told Patricia that we needed to leave EPIC and work on "The Rock". What was it going to be, a men's retreat as I had originally thought, no I said standing looking out the window over the property and towards my son's house, I said no, we are to " **Focus on the Family** ".

A few hours later I got a call out of blue, he said, " Hi, my name is Mark and I am with **Focus on the Family**." (I had golfed in a charity tournament with him a few years before and told him about The Rock and he stopped by once for coffee a year or two ago). He said, " I am going to be in Kelowna on Weds and am bring the President of Focus on the Family with me and would love to bring him up to " The Rock" and have you share your vision with him." Wow, I had just said those words a few hours before, and so far told no one except Patricia, what Godly timing.

I had coffee with both of my sons who have both left their churches and presently not attending or in between and they loved the idea and wanted to help. I talked to my 13 yr old grandson, who is likely the inspiration for all this as he is presently not attending any church or youth group either and I would love to see him get involved and grow in his relationship with GOD and not just drift away. He will be going to University in 4 years, time is short. I asked him if he would like to help me form some type of ministry here on our property. He loved the idea and said he is just reading a book about a pastor who left the structured church to start something like that. Wow, GOD in action or what. GOD is working in everyone's lives and it is amazing when it all comes together in a moment, better than magic, it is our GOD.

There has been alot going on behind the scenes with me at EPIC for the past few months, much of it I cannot explain. I will not go into details but can say I believe it was just GOD working and preparing me and others to enable our exit. My thoughts have been in overdrive with the Vision night coming up and as I wrote down all my thoughts and dreams, it was obvious my heart had moved from EPIC to The Rock.

In the past 3 years I have enjoyed and learned more at EPIC in my spiritual walk than any time before. Pastor Monty could take a bible story I have heard hundreds of time and make come alive anew with applications I had never heard or thought of before. We love the EPIC tribe and will continue with many of them as lifelong friends.

Many have asked why you can't do The Rock with EPIC. I say because I need to pour all my energy into The Rock, if I stay at EPIC and will see a need, I will just naturally step up and help. I cant do both. Also, I believe what GOD wants The Rock to be a place for those disenfranchised from the church as a place to come back and meet together, to have fellowship and reunite their relationship with GOD.

If I asked my son to come to church with me, he would say no. When I asked him if he wanted to help me build The Rock as a place for those who have left the church, his eyes lite up and he glowed with an enthusiast YES !!! I have talked to a few other friends who have left the structured church and they cant wait for us to start.

I pray you can see GOD's hand in all of this. When things happen you don't understand, I find it is time to look up and say " GOD, what are you up to and what are you trying to tell me ".

Then when HE tells, it is time to act.

We pray GOD's continued blessing on the EPIC tribe and look forward to coffees and maybe an occasional Sunday worship together as continue to "Grow the Kingdom".

107 . ON THIS ROCK , I will re-build my Church.

I was sitting having a coffee with Patricia on our deck and *GOD said to me, " Oh by the way, I killed that tree that was in your way. You can now go ahead with the building of The Rock that was stopped."*

I looked down to the tree I knew HE was talking about and couldn't see it because a big fir tree was in my line of site. The tree was a very unusual white birch not common to this area but when I lived up north they were everywhere. The guy that lived here before me planted many unique trees.

When I was first building things for "The Rock" I had envisioned an outdoor ping pong table in this perfect spot and a sand box for the little kids nearby. I took the bobcat down there and realize this tree was right in the middle of where I wanted the ping pong table.

No problem, I will just dig out an area to the east of it and carry on. I started to dig and we hit "The Rock". We uncovered a few 100 sq ft of it but it was very much in the way and sloping at a 45 degree angle so no way to do what I wanted without either back filling to level which would have buried the rock and also buried the tree.

So I just left the area and have been concentrating efforts for the past few years on the other side of the house.   **I was curious, had GOD really killed that tree ?**

Coffee break was over and we were going out for dinner with Jim & Jeanne at 5:30. I really wanted to **finish** the rose garden on the other side of the house before we had to clean up and head out.

All it needed was one or two more bobcat loads, level and it would be finished. BUT .... we are NOT allowed to use the "F" word up Gramps house I tell the grandkids. They laugh as they know I mean the word "Finish".

Why call "finish" the "F" word? Here is why, last count we have 98 projects underway at The Rock. If I allow myself, which is my nature, to get so focused on finishing various projects, we will miss out on relationship opportunities. Good example... the two grandboys and I had just completed a move of a nice family and I was dropping them off at their house. It was about 5:00 pm and Alicia met us on the driveway and invited me to join them for supper. She said they had put some extra burgers on the BBQ as they knew we would be hungry after the move. I said, "No, I have this project at home that is almost finished and need to get home so I can finish it before dark." Ouch, turn down supper with my son's family and build relationship so I can finish some project that I can do any other day.

I said, "Ops, not allowed to say the "F" word," and I had a wonderful supper with them including my grandchildren and some of their friends.

OK, going back to coffee break and whether I go check out the tree or rush back to finish the rose garden. I am so glad that I chose to check out the tree. I wandered down to where the tree was and sure enough, it was dead.

Then GOD said," I want you to move the key area of The Rock back here to this area, because on this rock, I am going to re-build my Church." This is affirming our desire to reach out to those that have been disenfranchised or left the historical church structure and give them a place where they can re-connect.

I said that is awesome, will do, but said that I was sad that the unique tree had to die, so the plan for The Rock could live.

GOD said," I fully understand how it is heartbreaking that something, SOMEONE you love has to die so that others can live."

My 7 encounters with GOD

on my journey thru the

HOLY LAND.

108: ***ISREAL,***

 We were on a seven day bus tour of Israel in 2015 and were driving up from the coast when I saw the road sign.

"TO JERUSALEM."

The spiritual emotions that this road sign awoke in me is indescribable. I was on my way to Jerusalem, the city of GOD. What history, what a future. GOD would meet with me seven times on this trip and challenged me to my core.

It is one thing to read or hear various Bible stories as I have all my life, but a totally different experience to be there. Standing where they stood, smelling the air, experiencing the culture and see the whole panorama of the land and how everything interacts with everything else.

My favourite Bible Character and person I likely relate to the best is Elijah.

What a great story. You can read it in the Bible under 1 Kings, in chapters 17 & 18. ***"How long will you go limping between the two sides ? If Jehovah be GOD, follow him; but if Baal, then follow him. And the people answered him not a word."***

So when we decided to go the Israel I thought I have to find Mount Carmel, climb to the top and if possible, *sleep overnight on the summit* and seek to spend that night with GOD.

The journey started in Athens, Greece. One of the oldest cities in the world and credited with being the foundation of democracy, philosophy and the Western Civilization.

Athens history is very much into Greek Mythology or I am sure they would be offended by the word "Myth" as they very seriously worshiped their many gods. Fearful of missing anyone, (political correctness of the 1st millennium BC generation) they built a temple on nearly every high hill.

Amazing architecture. How did they build such large buildings of beautifully sculptured stone. Then get it to the top of that mountain. They pointed out the rock quarry which was up in the mountains way in the horizon. One column we saw somewhere was about 6 ft round and 60 ft high and made from one stone. There were about 24 columns that size in that structure of the most different and beautiful granite.

The Parthenon it is about a 100 ft wide. The length is 228 ft and height is 34 feet. Impressive as built in 447 BC. Inside was said to be a statue made of gold of the goddess Athena 60 feet high. Ok, I said this temple is only 34 ft high but she was in the previous temple destroyed in 480 BC. So that one must have been even greater. The Parthenon was a temple but also used as the countries treasury.

Your god is only as good shown by your wealth and power.

They said on festivals, over 100,000 people made their way up the long path below us up the mountain, then thru this one gate. Marble stone staircases are not a good idea, way to slippery. Before them would have went the priests and maybe 10,000 oxen or other animal for sacrifice. Didn't see any portapotties.

Interesting how the worship of sex came into this journey. Many of the temples were to gods of fertility and that many of the rituals had to do with sex. Not a lot different today. Our church has taken on the task of helping men and families with "The Conquer Series". It is a program to help men break free from the addition of porn and the impact it has on their wives, family and job.
Porn is rampid in our society and even more so within the church. They say the stricter the rules, the more excess in the porn addiction. It is a secret place that you alone can control.

I stood on the rock where the Apostle Paul preached his sermon on " to an unknown God". A summary of Paul's message:

"People of Athens! I see that in every way you are very religious. For as I walked around and looked carefully at your objects of worship, I even found an altar with this inscription: to an unknown god. So you are ignorant of the very thing you worship—and this is what I am going to proclaim to you....

God did this so that they would seek him and perhaps reach out for him and find him, though he is not far from any one of us."

Yes, and I was looking forward to that and trying to know Him better. I was seeking and reaching out to GOD and trusting that He would meet me at my Holy Place on top of Mount Carmel. That was only a week away.

We went to Ephesus, One temple had a statue of a Roman standing with his right foot on a ball. I thought maybe he was the soccer champion but the inscription said. "He had control of the whole world under his right foot", it was a sphere, so when did we start believing the world was flat. Apparently from 2,000 BC to 200 AD when that statue was made, it was known to be a sphere.

So many things that I thought as a child to be the truth, or the right way to do it, or was "a sin", like dancing or drinking wine, turns out it was just someone trying to control something and somehow got everyone believing it. It makes me very skeptical. When I was young we got Government grants to install formaldehyde foam to insulate our houses, then later when it was found to be a major cancer thing killing people, we got Government grants to take it out.... who can you believe.

The library in Ephesus at one time was considered to be one of 3 largest in the world. Destroyed by an earthquake in about 250 AD. Interesting though, the brothel was just across the street and when they were excavating they found a secret tunnel going from the library to the brothel. I can just hear it now," Bye Dear, I am going down to the library for a few hours, don't wait up."

Times have not changed much.

After Greece and Turkey we visited Dubai. I had some really good chats with some local Emiratees about their faith. I heard that a really important thing is that you pray. It is something to see the whole country stop 5 times a day to pray. The loud speakers are everywhere so no matter where you are, you hear it. Erie chant like sound, very beautiful.

I have often wondered, there are some 1.5 billion Muslin and about 1.0 billion Hindu in the world. To me, is Christianity "right" only because I was born in a Christian family? Could all those people be wrong or do I just not understand them sufficiently?

I wanted to ask him what he prayed about but didn't get the chance. I suppose if they are praying for wealth, they got it. The "prosperity gospel" is alive and doing EXTREMELY well in Dubai.

I saw a big Prayer Room sign in the big mall, never seen that in Christian English North American Mall.

Next we visited Israel.

109: MOUNT CARMEL

It was really ironic that my first stop in Israel was at a hotel named: "Herods, " after Herod the Great. The crazy man that killed all the babies when Jesus was born as he was worried a new king was born to over throw him. In his paranoia, he killed his own kids as he thought they were plotting to kill him and take over the throne. Maybe they were, it was done a lot in those days. He had 2,000 body guards.

We heard many stories about him the whole week in Israel. He built some amazing things during his reign from about 30 BC to 4 AD. Actually, he was not a Jew, he was an Arab. But he saw his opportunity and became friends with the Romans and had them appoint him King over Judah. (Jews) So, there is another reason the Jews didn't like him, but, because Rome was in charge at the time, they had to make it work.

We were on the tour bus heading to our next stop, at Haifa still about 30 km north of us where we would tour the Baha'i temple and stay the night. I had decided back home when I read that the tour of the Baha'i temple was on the itinerary that I would skip that. After all, why are we going to the Baha'i Temple on a Protestant tour of the Holy Land. It almost seemed inappropriate to me. I mean, their belief is so far from Christianity, it was about inclusive and tolerance of other and all religions. That all religions lead to god and we just need to live in peace and harmony, Kumbaya.

I was going to find a taxi and head up the Mountain to find Elijah's place because Haiti is built on Elijah's Mount Carmel.

Then while sitting on the bus looking out the window, I just happened to be on the mountain side, the other side had the sea view.

God spoke: **" Look up there, that is where it happened !"**
referring to the story of Elijah / God vs 350 Priest / Baal and calling down of fire from heaven to consume the offering place. The place I was looking for.

"No" I said, "you are wrong." OK, so how many people do you know that have told GOD HE was wrong. Not the smartest kid on the block but hey, that's what I said. I then said: "I have been studying this map and it shows the National Monument of Elijah is right here, (pointing to the map) about 30 km NW of where GOD was saying it was. It was by the coast and near the City of Haifa. Also, the map shows that that the location of Mount Carmel is up there and a special monument to Elijah too so it must be up there, not here. GOD ignored my comment, thank heavens.

Then GOD broke my heart. HE said, "I **am not going to meet you at Mount Carmel as you planned. But I would suggest you go see the Baha'i Temple."** And HE was gone.

I was ticked. I had travelled almost half way around the world to meet GOD at MY Holy Mountain and HE just breezes thru, said not gonna happen and by the way, instead of doing what you wanted to do, that which I had planned and dreamed of for months or even my whole life, rather, go do what you didn't want to do or even refused to do as it appalled me. Definitely not the first time GOD has had a different plan for me than I did. In the story about Cumberland Boys Club I said an absolute "NO" to that, but turned out to be one of the best things I have ever done.

I have often wondered why GOD puts up with me the way I talk to HIM sometimes. I think maybe HE likes my honest discussions. I am not afraid to talk to HIM like a friend, a real relationship, a two way street, not just a "yes" man. I am a Child of GOD and am instructed to come boldly before the throne. I know, sometime a little more respect would in order, but GOD knows my heart and is patient with me. **After all, HE is GOD and HE can take it**.

110:   Meeting with GOD at the Baha'I Temple, HE is not happy.

The tour bus pulled into Haifa. I didn't know it at the time as I was stewing over my cancelled meeting with GOD which did not go my way, but we drove right past the National Monument to Elijah. If I would have been paying attention I would have seen the big signs and the place.

How much have I missed out on just because I was distracted by my own selfish wants.

We stopped at the Baha'i Temple. This garden goes from the base of Mount Carmel to the top. Wow can't believe that, MY holy mountain has been taken over by them. I just wanted to shout :

"GET OFF MY MOUNTAIN !   "

GOD had suggested to me that I should visit the Baha'i Temple, much against my plans and desires. Now when GOD suggests something, it is a good idea to do it.

As the tour bus pulled up to the front gate of the Temple, I debated, do I do as I had planned for months and had told Patricia that I was going to leave the tour and find a taxi to take me to where Elijah had called down the fire from heaven, or go into the temple. I was sure I could get a taxi from the Baha'i Temple as it was the main tourist attraction of the area. I really didn't know why this Temple was on a "Protestant tour" anyway, especially when we were right there in Elijah territory.

I thought of the day before at the Port of Jaffa. The port where Jonah had caught his boat to run away from what GOD had wanted him to do and that was go to the city of Nineveh. We all know that did not work too well for Jonah and he ended up in Nineveh anyway. So, I told Patricia that I was going to reluctantly go with her and tour the (inferred by attitude "stupid") temple.

So I went in, but to add insult to my attitude already, this sign was at the gate, **"Baha'i Holy Place".** This was my Holy Place... and I was not happy to share it with them.

The Guide mentioned that there was only about 15 more minutes to go into the temple and then it would be closed to the public. I thought, well, too bad, I guess I didn't make it... Then re-thought, I have 15 minutes, I better at least try. I did make it and when I got inside, took the time to read their Manifest.

It is my understanding that they believe that all roads or faiths lead to GOD, that you need to love, live in peace, look after the earth and have tolerance and be inclusive.

I wandered out of the temple and around the corner of the courtyard when: **GOD grabbed me, spun me around and said in a most disgusted tone,"this is like My Church ! "**

And again, GOD was gone.

Wait I thought, what do you mean? You can't just blow in here and blast off what is really annoying you and leave. I am not even sure what you mean.

GOD would take the time to explain, but not here, and not yet. I had much more to see and learn. When HE did explain, it was much greater and personal than I ever wanted to hear.

111: MOUNT CARMEL, I went looking anyway.

I did get to sleep at the top of Mount Carmel. It has a changed a little in the past 3,000 years. A major roadway goes all the way along the top of it. Turns out Mount Carmel is more of a very long hog back type coastal mountain range. Stretches from the Mediterranean Sea and then down the middle of Israel for 40 km.

We got to the Hotel and I was thrilled that I would get one of my dreams of sleeping on top of Carmel, but not under the stars but in a really nice Hotel. In that GOD said HE wasn't coming to chat there was no sense in being uncomfortable. After supper I figured that I have travelled halfway around the world to visit the place that Elijah called down fire, I am going there. According to the map, I might just be a block or two away from the national Monument to Elijah so Patricia and I went for a walk to find it.

I went to the front desk and asked for a map and asked if they knew where the spot was. Oh yes, just down the road, about a 5 minute taxi ride. I checked into what he said and realized that was just Elijah's cave, where he likely mentored Elisha and not the actually fire from heaven place. So I asked the concierge and he didn't know what I was talking about. Asked a taxi driver and he got another guy, I was getting a royal run around and getting very frustrated. WHY, we are on the top of Mount Carmel does not any of these tourist people know the most important thing about this place. AAARRRGGGGGGGGGGGGGG !!!

Finally, someone said, oh, you mean "Scorched Earth". YES... that is it, I had read that in one of the books. Can you take me there? It is about 30 KM to the SE of here and there is not point, it is closed to the public now. Oh man, 30 km to the SE, right where GOD had pointed it out to me when I was on the bus. Go figure HE'd be right and I would be wrong. Not only wrong, but HE told not to bother going but I had to press to the point of total frustration. Should have just listened in the first place.

Ok, calm down Deryl. It is not meant to be, accept it.

Patricia said "lets go for a walk as we had seen a lovely view point overlooking the city and sea just on the backside of the hotel". We did and walked along the top ridge of the mountain. As we looked over the city, now nearly dark I could see a small cloud coming up from the sea and moving very fast our way. It was dark all around but the sun was still shining on this cloud. I was amazed. Just like when Elijah had finished and GOD proved HE was GOD and all the people shouted; "Jehovah, He is GOD, Jehovah, He is GOD." and all of Israel fell down and turned from Baal and worshiped Jehovah.

Then Elijah prayed and a small cloud came up out from the sea onto Mount Carmel and Elijah told them to prepare for rain. It had not rained for years as they had a terrible drought.

The next morning when we woke up it was raining. One of the only rains we had on our 35 day trip. The other was in St. Petersburg, such irony, the only two places I really wanted to see was Mount Carmel and St. Petersburg and it rained in both places. More on that in meeting #6, yeah, GOD mets me in Russia but won't on Mt Carmel. Go figure.... sometime I just can't figure out HIS logic.

We got on the bus and it stopped raining. The tour guide got on and said, " I trust you will endure this rain we had last night as it is very unusual at this time of year and it has been so dry up here, they are suffering from a drought and the area really needed it. " Like a miracle I think he said. Your welcome, I thought to myself and thanked GOD for such a little detail that would normally not even be recognized, but was truly a blessing, especially for me right then and there.

112: NAZERETH

On our way to Nazareth. Can anything good come out of Nazareth, they say. I can see that, kind of like the Rutland of Kelowna (I can say that I am from Rutland and proud of it) or Surrey or Cumberland of BC. Rough town, high in the hills, a worker man's town. The answer is obvious, YES. Sometimes we are too quick to judge, I am anyway.

This was Jesus's home from when he was about 6 when they had come back from Egypt until he was about 20 I understand.

Outside our guide pointed down the valley, as Nazareth is on a hill top. Almost all the towns in Israel are built on the hills. The valley is for crops. A ridge about 2,000 to 3,000 ft high goes down the middle of Israel with a plain on the west to the Mediterranean (the 2,000 ft side) and beautiful flat valley to the east where the Jordan river flows. (the 3,000 ft side as the Jordon is about 1,000 ft below Sea level)

Anyway, the guide pointed out it is over 130 km from here to Bethlehem, where the very pregnant Mary and Joseph travelled and then gave birth to Jesus in Bethlehem. To my amazement, a man, about my age asked, "why did they go all the way to Bethlehem to have the baby, why didn't they just have him here?" Wow, I could not believe someone my age (in 60's) didn't know the answer to that, it is so basic... to me. I am not criticizing the man but rather having to re-think, not everyone knows the story.

The bus toured around the city of Nazareth, there was a hillside near Jesus's house, I could just visualize the boy Jesus and his buddies playing on this hill. Not sure if they played cowboys and Indians like we did or hide and go seek. So how do you hide from Jesus ?

As we know, Jesus was teaching in the Synagogues and amazing the Rabbi's from when he was young, one story of when He was just 12. Well, there is a synagogue just across the street from Jesus childhood home and he must have talked and discussed things a lot there. We know from Jesus's teaching that it was extremely radical from the Jewish old testament type teachings of the day. So radical in fact, in Nazareth they tried to kill him by throwing him off a cliff. He ended up walking thru the crowd untouched but realized that a Prophet is not accepted in his own town, so decided to move.

Now this is interesting as I learned something new and so far, no western Christian I have asked has know this, but it makes total sense but not sure if true. Our Guide has his degree in Israel history, great passion for his work, life of Christ and so knowledgeable. When we questioned him on some of the info he had he stated it comes from the Bible but also various letters written and other books and documents that they have.

A Mother down in Capernaum on the Sea of Galilee heard of Jesus's amazing teaching and desired that her son be discipled or mentored by such a Rabbi (teacher). She heard he was kicked out of Nazareth so she invited him to come stay with them. Her son is Peter. Wow. Blow me away. Does that every make sense. So build on that. Jesus hikes down the hill about 20 km and lived on the sea of Galilee from when he was about 20 until his ministry started at about age 30 and (maybe) lives with Peter and his family.

We visited Peter's house. It is right on the beach, about 30 feet from the Sea of Galilee, perfect for a fisherman. He had his boat and nets tied up right out front his door. Now for Jesus, perfect too, because just outside the back door and across the street is the synagogue.

We asked, how we know this is Peter's house? Our Guide said, we have letters from early century Christians. They were being persecuted so when they traveled, there was this letter that had a map showing the location and design of a safe house if they were in Capernaum. This was one marked as Peter's Mother.

So if Jesus stayed at this house from age 20 to 30, He must have spoken and chatted in the synagogue across the street. In that it is a small town I am sure he knew everyone and they knew him. I bet that Andrew and the rest of the young teens hung out with this awesome and radical Rabbi. They were likely a "Band of Brothers". Jesus likely told them that one day he would start his ministry and go preach throughout Israel. I am sure Peter's Mom & Dad overheard all this and approved over the supper and while celebrating the Sabbath table.
Then one day Peter is mending his nets and Jesus comes along and says, the time has come for me to start my ministry to all of Israel, are you in? Peter drops his net and says I am in, lets do it !

This makes so much more sense than what I have always thought where Jesus goes walking along the sea shore one day, bumps into Peter, a total stranger and asks him to join him, to make him, a fisher of men. Peter says yes, leaves his Dad and the fishing business high and dry. Now I can see that Peters Mom and Dad were in on it all along and rather than the western style of "Be saved and save the world" there was 10 years of mentoring and preparation.
A RELATIONSHIP was formed first.

My most favorite spot on the whole trip was sitting on **<u>a rock</u>** by the Sea of Galilee just outside Peter's house. We sat under a tree and just imagined Peter, the guys and Jesus mending their nets and laughing together, talking and even maybe planning their lives and journey ahead. If the guys had only REALLY known what was ahead, but that all came in time and place as they learned and grew spiritually.

Just like today.

113: A BAPTISM in the River Jordan

The day before we got to the River Jordan a few on the bus were talking about being baptized in the river. I had thought of it but questioned my motives as I have been baptised already once by my brother Lloyd in water and once by GOD in blood. I talked to the various guys that had said they would like to do it, and I must say, I judged them and did not find them worthy or should I say didn't feel their motives were appropriate. Definitely being brought up as a good Baptist, they would NOT have qualified. After-all, they had not attended any baptism classes or even made any declaration of their faith.

I felt they wanted to get baptized in the Jordan as it would be a mega tick beside their spiritual quest. They not only got baptized, but in the Jordan River, GOD would surely take that into account. Definitely tempting to have that on my Spiritual resume but not the right reason. They did get baptized in the Jordan and it was a beautiful ceremony to behold.

We travelled the road between Jericho and Jerusalem. I couldn't help but remember the story of the Good Samaritan as we looked at that dusty windy hilly road. There were many tents along the way, tribesman whose ancestors likely lived there then.

One day the bus stopped by a dusty old dirt road and we got out and stood there waiting for our guide to say where we were. You are standing on the Emmaus Road he said. I wept.

We also went to the creek where David picked his stones to slay Goliath on the hillside behind us. Amazing. The guide pointed down the valley to the horizon, some 20 miles. He said that is Bethlehem, where David had walked from to bring his brothers some food.

Just to stand there...

114: Sailed on the SEA OF GALILEE

We went out on an old wooden boat onto the Sea of Galilee. It was awesome. To visualize the shoreline where Jesus prepared the fish for the guys. It was right around here where Jesus walked on the water, and Peter did too.

We fished, didn't catch anything. No we didn't try the other side. I think they might have been scared they would have caught more than they could handle. After-all, they had 32 people on a chartered cruise and a restricted time schedule to maintain. Catching more fish than they could handle just **would NOT work into that schedule.**

Sound familiar???

While we were on the boat, a sparrow came and sat beside me. I took his picture. **His eye is on the sparrow, and I know HE watches me.**

We visited the chapel where Jesus performed his first miracle at a wedding turning the water into wine. We decided to renew our wedding vows at the chapel on this property.

There were rocks everywhere, a perfect size for holding in your hand, just a little bigger than your fist, an off white. (appropriate color) It was custom of Jesus's day that if someone was caught doing something wrong, you stoned them to death. Right then and there. Can you imagine that? These were small towns and you would think they most likely knew everyone and were probably closely related. The rock feels so comfortable in my hand, just like it was meant to be thrown.

To be so quick to judge, and to judge to the point of killing.

I brought a stone home to remind me. Not to be judged by people so much but also and **since I got the rock,** not to be so quick to judge.

To use "The Rock" to build with, not to destroy.

Talking about judging what is right and wrong, what is the law? More important is it better to KEEP the LAW or is it better to keep the INTENT of the LAW?

We drove past some pastures, some had beautiful crops and others were in dirt, while others were wild.   We were told that 2015 (the year we were there) or in the Jewish calendar it is the year 5,775 which divides by 7 so is the "Shmita" or "Sabbatical Year". You are not to work the fields with the idea of letting them rest, rejuvenate. Our guide said that the Jewish farmers go to the Rabbi and say, " I will not be working my fields this year" and they get a certificate, a tick mark beside their name for being good and obeying the law that they " will not be working the field that year."

Then some farmers turn around and lease their land out to an Arab for a year, who does work the land.   The Rabbi most likely gets paid for his work, record keeping and blessing. The Arab makes money from the harvest and the Jew makes money from the lease.   All should be good, the letter of the law was followed, everyone came out richer. Richer in money that is if,

money is the end goal?

115: Jerusalem. The Holy City of GOD.
JERUSALEM....SUNDAY MORNING.

How appropriate to started our Sunday on the Mount of Olives overlooking the valley with the Garden of Gethsemane and the old city wall of Jerusalem with the Eastern Gate just behind. One day, this mountain will split in two as the KING of Kings and LORD of Lords returns to set up HIS Kingdom on this earth and enter triumphantly thru that gate.

When Jesus arrived at this same place 2,000 years ago on his fateful trip into Jerusalem, He stopped and looked over the city and wept for it, like I was. At this point He reached a major cross roads in His journey, a fork in the road. He could go right and go back home to his friends and family and have a good business as a Rabbi or teacher as he had many followers, or He could go left, to His death. Without hesitation, He chose to go left, which was GOD's will and Jesus' purpose.

In the valley below are thousands of crypts, 150,000 to be exact. (a crypt is a cement or stone burial tombs above ground). They want to be first to rise when Christ returns at that place. The Guide pointed some out, see the crypt with the very pointed dome, that is where Absalom, David's sons is buried. There is Josaphat's crypt, and the prophet ... and ... as he names off many of the names from the Bible we have heard. So amazing and brought all those names to real life.

We went from the Mount of Olives to Gethsemane, which is in the valley just below between the Mount of Olives and the Old City wall. A beautiful garden, with olive trees said to be over 2,000 years old. It was said that these were the same trees as when Jesus came here to pray.

The garden is in the middle of the big city. Dozens of tour buses but it was still such a quiet and peaceful place. I wandered the garden and came to the rock where Jesus prayed just before he would be betrayed by His friend and "treasurer" or money man, Judas. I got to kneel at the rock in Gethsemane where Jesus prayed, "Not my will but GOD's be done" as the **anguish** of what He was to do and go thru had Him sweating drops of blood.

We then went thru the Gate and into the old city. As we approached the gate, I heard the Spirit tell me to remove my ear phones (which we had to hear the Guide) because HE (the Spirit) would be my guide today. I needed to stay focused, no distractions.

I removed my ear phones and the Guide started to give some instructions so I put it back in. The ear phones immediately went dead. Stupid battery, I did charge it last night. Patricia saw me fretting so offered me hers. I refused but she insisted as she said I remember the stories better. I put hers on that she had been using and within a few steps, it too went dead.

Patricia mentioned it to the Guide and he had a spare one, so he gave it to me. Wanna guess what happened... yeah, it too worked for about a minute and then went dead. I don't know why GOD bothers with me, I am a little slow to listen but I finally put them all away and just focused. Also too embarrised to tell Patricia that GOD told me not to use earphones so played along just to have GOD kill 3 sets.

We wandered thru the narrow streets and then came to a large opening, it was the Wailing Wall. I really didn't care for the Wailing Wall. Not my style. You are supposed to go up and put your prayer on a piece of paper and put it in a crack in the giant stone wall. No thanks.

I know I can pray anywhere, any time, **pray without ceasing.** I appreciate that this is the only remaining part of Solomon's original temple which housed the Holy of Holies, where GOD did reside over 2,000 years ago. But when Jesus died, the big curtain that separated the Holy of Holies where only the High Priest was allowed to go in and meet with GOD was torn in half, top to bottom, (GOD to me) and **allowing me to boldly come before GOD anywhere, anytime.** I should limit my telling HIM HE is wrong though and watch I do not take my boldness for granted.

So I just hung back. I put on my beany hat on as required and watched the Jewish men in their fancy Jewish attire weep, weave and wail. I was thinking, too bad you guys just don't except Jesus as your Messiah, life would a lot better for you. You're really missing out with all your rules, laws and traditions.

At the same time I found myself being drawn closer to the wall. At a few feet away, an opening formed against the normally eerie crowded wall, and **GOD spoke:"Come, touch My wall and meet with ME here."**

I came forward and placed both my hands on the wall and stood just inches away. A flood overcame me as a filling of the Holy Spirit came over me and a bird flew between me and the wall. There was only inches so it's wings pressed against my chest as it flew by.

I stayed there for some time and I too, wept against the wall.

116: I climbed the hill of CALVARY to the CROSS:

Most of my life I have dreamt and visualized the day I would walk up the hill to Calvary.

That Sunday, I did it.

We left the Wailing Wall and walked the narrow crowded walkway to the courtyard where Jesus had his court case. We wandered past the courtyard, past the whipping post where I could not imagine the pain as those whips shredded His body to almost the point of death and being unrecognizable from all the blood. We went to the outer courtyard and then to the Via Dolorosa. The road to the cross.

The way is about 2,000 feet up a windy stone path to the top of Calvary or Golgotha just out of the City where they took the criminals to die what is said to be a most torturous horrible death being nailed to a cross. We passed the place where Jesus fell and a Roman Guard grabbed Simon and had him carry Jesus's cross. Custom was that a Roman soldier could ask you to carry his armour (or whatever) for a mile and you had to. Jesus taught that if you are asked to carry it a mile, carry it two.

The procession to this point was very solemn and quite. There maybe thousands on this journey with you but you seem alone. Then about halfway, merchants appear on both sides of the narrow pathway. They are selling trinkets, soccer balls with "Jesus Loves you" on them, crosses of every description and mainly Christ cross orientated junk and calling out to you to come in.

I had been warned by many about this and told that you really need to keep your focus.

The noise level grows as you climb.
The crowds get larger and people are pushing.
At times it is so narrow from the merchant's things you can barely pass.

I totally lost my focus and became frustrated.

Finally we reached the top of Calvary, top of Golgotha. I saw no hill, all I saw was stores and then this big dirty old church. Sorry if I have ruined your journey with me but hang in there, GOD shows up.

We got into the church and Patricia was done. She said she would just stay at the door and wait for me. It was 40 degrees Celsius or 104 Fahrenheit outside and the church had no air conditioning. I almost did the same but decided to join the long Disney like line that meandered up steep old stone steps to the cross.

I finally got to the position of the cross but the Orthodox had got their first. If hanging one lamp is good, hang a hundred. If one Icon plaque is good, place thousands. **So many you cannot see Jesus but just see all the "STUFF"! (sometimes we are like that with whatever our "stuff" is from things, rules or just life.)**

Under an Alter, a table like any church communion table but very ornate and likely gold, you can crawl underneath, one at a time and see under a 2'x2' Plexiglas the rock. Said to be the rock where the cross was, which was cracked from the earthquake.

By now, I am very sinister and DONE. I am finding no spiritual awakening or blessing as I was expecting to be totally wasted in tears at this point.

Instead I am disgusted by the zoo.

I passed a rock slab where it is said that they washed Jesus the Christ's body on after the crucifixion. People were lined up kneeing on it and wailing, I cannot judge, they were on their journey, bless them.

Then I wandered thru the crowded room to the holy tomb or crypt. It looks like solid brass, maybe gold, don't know, don't care. I pressed my way around the right side and to the back where numerous caves in the rock or tombs were displayed. I did not get in the big line up to go into the brass crypt.

Priests would come out and waive their lanterns with incense and chant something, seemed more like the dolls coming out of the clock at Small-world in Disneyland to me.

Totally frustrated and annoyed I tried to make my way back to the front door to find Patricia and just leave. We could wait outside for the rest. It was very difficult going against the wailing crowd which was moving towards the crypt.

Then I saw it. A movement from in front of the crypt. It was like someone was trying to work their way thru the crowd and come to where I was. I could see the crowd jostling around as this unseen energy force weaved it way thru the people. Back and forth and you could see people being moved by it so it could push its way thru, not a straight line, but around one person one way then around another the other way.

Finally it got to me, again, **it was GOD !** Just like at the Baha'i Temple HE spun me around and pinned me to the wall and just like at the Baha'i Temple HE was very annoyed and frustrated too. **He said, "See, *this is what I was talking about at the Baha'i Temple, this is what is wrong with my church today !!!*"**

And again, HE was gone.

But this time HE would not be gone for long and next time we met, HE explained everything and HE had a lot to say.

117: GOD speaks HIS mind on Mount Calvary

We got back to the Hotel which was located very close to, if not on, Mount Calvary. It was a very long and amazing Sunday. Aside from the frustration at the cross, overall the day was the best day of my life.

I had settled in **and GOD showed up**. Impossible for me to explain but I know it is HIM as HIS Spirit is talking to my spirit. I believe my spirit is me. It was like HE was sitting in the easy chair, very comfortable and definitely not in a rush to move on this time, but to sit down and really chat.

Chat is likely the wrong word as I don't recall getting a word in as I was afraid to speak. I know many are skeptical of this whole story, I was too, but I ask you to follow along thru to meeting #7 where GOD absolutely clarifies this all to true and that HE is GOD.

This is what God said. I may not remember the exact words but the content is true. Like most of these stories, I wrote them down right away so I wouldn't forget, collection of over 25 years.
(things in brackets are things I put in to explain background)
****
GOD said: *" So, you have some questions for ME, well let me give you some answers.*

First, I told you that I was not going to meet with you as you had planned on Mount Carmel. Let ME explain. Mount Carmel should have been the redemption mountain, the salvation story and we should have never needed to have Mount Calvary and MY Son to die.

You see, MY people, the Jews of the day, had turned away from ME again and started to worship the god Baal. (It is my understanding that Baal was seen as the god of fertility, both for man and for harvest. He ruled the rain and fire, two very important and needed things). *We needed a total turn around and get all of Israel back to being MY people.*

Well, people have always been impressed with miracles. Show me ! They say. So we went for the biggest. Baal and his 350 priests were supposed to be in control of the rain, I proved them wrong as I stopped the rain for many years and nothing they could do about it. Then with the big showdown on Mount Carmel with the challenge which god could bring down fire to consume the offering, the priest of Baal and Baal totally failed. They cut themselves and everything, Elijah got a little mouthy by mocking them saying maybe Baal was asleep, maybe on a journey, maybe you should shout louder. Possibly got a little out of hand, much like someone else I know. Eh Deryl ?

I then brought down the fire and as you know from looking for the place called "Scorched Earth" with MY fire from heaven I consumed the offering, all the water poured on it and even the rocks themselves. So much for Baal being the god of fire.

Next I had Elijah pray and I sent rain. You know the rest of the story. Elijah prayed "so these people will know that you, Lord, are GOD, and that YOU are turning their hearts back again."

BUT... what do we have there today ? The International Head Quarters of the Baha'i faith. You would have thought Mount Carmel would have become the Holy Mountain where all repented and turned back to ME and the whole world followed, forever. But no, it was not long before they were back to worshiping other gods.

The problem is, if you give them a great miracle, they ohh and ahh, then ask for a bigger one. If you don't do it, they move on to the next "trend", the next thing or the next exciting movement. That applies to MY Church today too.

So I don't really care for Mount Carmel anymore. That is why I have met you here on the real Holy Mountain, in Jerusalem. Where the miracle that happened here, once and for all time, Jesus, truly saves, redeems and makes the ONLY way to re-unite our relationship.

When I said that the Baha'i faith was like my church, what I meant was they are more focused on things, image, being nice, tolerance and inclusion more than on having a relationship with ME. That is why I created you (mankind) but you (especially you Deryl) get so distracted by things and image and lose your focus on ME.

At the Cross and Tomb again I said it frustrated ME. You saw me walk thru that crowd. I bumped into many people, the irony of it, these people had come all the way to Calvary seeking ME, like they come to church, but when I bumped right into them, they went around ME so they could finish their pilgrimage which they had set as their goal. They were focused on the slab, or the rock, or the empty tomb, but not seeing ME.

Again, they missed the relationship with ME as they were focused on achieving the spiritual mission they had set for themselves.

But I didn't come to talk to you about others. They are all on their own journeys and I am dealing with each of them in their own way. I came to talk about you.

(Figuratively HE sat up in HIS chair and stared me in the eye. You want the hair on your neck to stand on end, just get the feeling GOD is staring you down)

I am upset with you.
YOU ARE MORE BAHA'I THAN CHRISTIAN !!!

(I tried to reply but didn't dare)

No... you would say and that you believe in God and Christ ...
You speak a great talk and even live a pretty good life....
But I know you from your HEART and you honestly believe I did it all wrong.

Your little comment about the Elijah place being 30 km north up by Haifa and saying I was wrong when I said it was right over there is trivial compared to your heart believing that MY method of salvation is wrong. That it is barbaric and likely is only just one of the ways to God.

You are very comfortable in the Christian community. You like the life style. There are nice people, some maybe a little to fanatical but you would totally lose your position in the church and lose face with your friends if you would say that Christ maybe isn't the only way. Maybe there are others, you would love to find a way to prove that all religions do lead to ME.

Don't deny it.... I know you, you can't fancy talk Me. (I didn't try)

Last night, you and Patricia had dinner with a Hindu couple that I set you up with. At the end of the dinner the man said, " Do you really believe that Jesus is truly the ONLY WAY ?". You didn't say a word, as you knew you couldn't. Patricia did. She spoke up right away and said it very well I might add. She's is great girl, I gave her to you as a gift, your sole-mate. I gave her to you as you need her and you should listen to what she has to say, especially when it comes to spiritual things. I love that girl's heart.

She spoke in very diplomatic so as "not to offend" but in a firm way. She said: " I didn't say it, Jesus said it. Jesus said, I am the way, the truth and the life, no man comes to the Father but by me." In that Hindu's see Jesus as a prophet or at least as a very wise man, how could they say anything after that. Nothing works better than quoting GOD's (My) word in a spiritual battle.

Lets talk about that further. You really don't like MY salvation plan, you think I could have done it better somehow that would have been more inclusive, maybe more tolerant, more acceptable. You don't <u>understand</u> why I did it that way.

Let ME tell you something, like I told Job.... Where were you when I created the world? You think you have to fully understand everything, think it thru and come to logical conclusion. Then explain to ME how the uncountable number of stars hang in space, explain to ME the boundaries of the universe, explain to ME infinity, or time, or even such a simple thing that you do all the time and that is "thought". You can't even start to explain any of it, and I haven't even gotten to the hard stuff yet.

My ways are higher than your ways,
My thoughts than your thoughts.
There is some scripture for you, Heard that before?

Today, you walked to the courtyard where my Son was whipped nearly to death and then you walked up the path to the Calvary where He was in such pain and agony He fell under the weight of it all. By the way, <u>we did not lose our focus going up that hill</u>. Then you went to the top of Mount Calvary to the place of the cross and Jesus's cruel death where He took on all the sins of the world, past, present and future. Even yours, Deryl.

<u>Do you think that if there would have been ..."another way"... we would have done all that... for you</u> ?

I, and I alone am GOD ! I created all things and ways for a reason, and Jesus is the way I chose to reunite the relationships between ME and YOU. I do not have to explain it to you. All you have to do is believe.   That, my friend, is what is called:

<u>FAITH.</u>

118: #6, GOD wanted to chat in Russia, of all places.

We got off the cruise ship in Saint Petersburg and were going on a tour to see the Winter Palace of Catherine the Great and the Hermitage Museum.

My history with Russia is interesting. (dates are close but I didn't look them up) Catherine the Great in 1763 offered land to the very productive German Mennonites after she had taken over the southern plains. My forefathers being Mennonites moved near the Crimean peninsula. Then July 15, 1878 they left Russia due to religious differences to the USA. My Dad's folks settled in Kansas and Mom's along with Patricia's family in Dakota's. Moved to Sask in 1900-1910 then to BC about 1943.

On July 15, 1998 my son Chris, 120 years to the day, left Canada and returned to Russia, very near the same area to teach in the schools, "Christian Morals and Ethics". We left because of religious persecution and returned to teach our religion. I went over for a few weeks to visit him. I have written some of the amazing stories in this book and hope to get the rest written one day.

Back to the story.
We got in the customs line in St Petersburg and things were going well. When it was Patricia and my turn we went up together like we have at every customs office. I was sternly told to get back in line as it was to only be one at a time. Ok, I went back. Strange though, as the family in front of us went up as 3 and the couple before them together. But I will not make waves, I am in Russia and don't want trouble.

I got back in line and a Russian Guard in uniform marched over and pushed me back as I had my toes over the red line. He waved his baton at my feet and glared at me saying to stay behind the line.

OK, I just obeyed. I was in line 2 and I noticed the guy in line 1 was totally over the line. Oh well, leave it alone.

Patricia was done and moved on and the green light came on. I stepped forward just to feel the push again of that Russian on my chest pushing me behind "the line". He motioned to the guy in line 1 to use my line and customs officer. Strange.

Then when he went on, I stepped forward just to get the Russian push back again. He ordered the lady in Line 1 to go. I mentioned about my wife and got a stern look and told he didn't care, I was to wait.

I noticed that line 4 had totally cleaned out and the light was green, so I wandered over there. I waited for the Customs guard to waive me on and started forward. That Russian had rushed over to my line now and stopped me again. He had the party in line 3 go, then he asked the third and fourth person, the rest of line 3 to step in front of me.

I bit my tongue and didn't say a word. I am sure my German face said it all.

The Guard wandered back to his desk by line #1 and I noticed in the next room there were 8 lines free. I looked and the guard was distracted so I snuck over into the other room, waited behind the red line to get the nod from the customs officer and advanced. In the corner of my eye I saw my Russian buddy come flying thru the door, I handed my passport to the customs officer and the Russian Guard realized he was too late and went back.

That took about an hour. Meanwhile Patricia was wondering where I was. There was likely 30 or more tour busses picking up people from the various cruise ships, like us, and almost all had left. Thanks heavens, ours waited but our tour would be shortened thanks to me.

Let me back up the story here a few days. Our first day on the cruise ship from Copenhagen to St Petersburg was at sea. We went to the Art Auction and I got mesmerized by a picture of a lion. I just couldn't take my eyes off it. Never experienced a painting feeling like that before. We had just come from Jerusalem, which is in Judah, and the Lion of Judah is Christ.

Back up a year and a meeting with my pastor. Our Platoon of guys, my nickname was "Squirrel", started when I gave my first talk introducing myself and I was telling who I was at about a "thousand words" a second (or fast anyway) and then hollered out " Squirrel !" and ran to the side. I felt I was talking to fast and had lost some so I wanted to see who was with me and who had seen the movie " UP ". A few laughed and it cleared the air.

Pastor Monty felt that with our new church plant, the nickname "Squirrel" was just not fitting what we needed to do. So he felt GOD had instructed him to rename me the " Lion". I didn't like it. I thought the title belongs to Christ and it is just too large a handle for me.

Back to the cruise ship. I really wanted that original painting. It cost a lot of money and then, where would I hang it, we have too many windows in our house and no wall space. We have dozens of pictures in the crawl space as no place to hang them. Then how do we get it home...

Finally I gave up and wandered back to my room. I opened my Ipad to get my best 5 pictures of the day to post on Facebook. The pictures on the Ipad went crazy and just ran thru the 1,852 pictures I had and settled on picture number about #100. It was a picture of me standing by a picture of a lion some 7 months before. Patricia said it was the same lion, how did I get it. I said we took it in Disneyworld back in Feb when we were there with the kids. It was a mural on a wall and I had it taken just for fun.

I now have it as my wallpaper on my cell and facebook to remind me. With the Lion of Judah behind me, I can do all things.

So, back to Russia. GOD shows up. Crazy, HE won't meet me in Israel on Mount Carmel but comes to Russia. Go figure.

GOD:" *I want to talk to you about that new wallpaper of the Lion you are using. If you are going to use it, believe it.*"

Me, in my defense which is really a stupid thing to do with GOD: "I do, what do you mean ? And by the way, what the heck was with that Russian Guard today. He did not bother anyone but me, it was so weird I figured YOU had to be behind this."

GOD: *Yes, it was. I wanted to show you something. You have that picture but I didn't see you really believing I had your back with that Russian Guard. You had your A, B and C plan going, no thought of ME.*

Let me remind you what believing really looks like.

I want to take you back to 1998 and at another Russian Customs office. Actually the only two times you have been in a situation like this and both in Russia.

You were going to visit your son Chris in Russia, your plane in Vancouver was delay which you knew you would miss your complicated connecting flights. Your reply. <u>I have total faith that if GOD wants these Bibles delivered, HE will get me there</u>.

You had asked Chris what he wanted you to bring, he said bibles. So you put the word out and you ended up with both your suitcases total full of only bibles. Nothing else could fit. You figured you could wear Chris's cloths when you got there.

You had talked with the Commission, the organization who your son was with, they said it was not a wise idea to take the bibles as Russia had just opened up and Bibles had been contraband for 70 years. These were still the same customs agents and what would likely happen is they would seize the bibles to review for propaganda material of which they would go into a warehouse and maybe never be seen again, and You would likely end up in a Russian jail and if you were lucky, be deported in a few weeks when your return ticket was due.

When you finally got to Moscow, it was about 2am and very long line ups at the customs. You went and filled out the usual customs form which they had told you to do before entering the line. They had every language and I had you picked German. When you finally got to the front, because you had filled the German form they put you in the German speaking line. When you said you could not speak any German they sent you back to fill out an English form and get to the back of the English line.

(so do you figure I wrote in tongues in German, as I did fill in the whole forms but I can't read or speak any German)

*You got to the back of the long English line at about 3am and no one else came in after that. Around 4am you were only 1 person away from the Customs Agent. (*Agent, they looked like KGB in full uniform and all had big guns). *All the other lines had finished and the Custom Agents had all wandered over to your line which was the only one left, then they could all go home.*

The guy in front of you was Middel Eastern and he had a very unusual box. You had noticed that they opened EVER suitcase and box, very thorough. When they would open yours, there was no hiding it was full of Bibles. BUT, you have said: <u>You never felt safer in your life, standing in a Russian customs line, as the only thing you had to rely on with everything going wrong, was me, GOD !</u>

About 16 fully armed KGB looking agents and then the guy in front of you goes ballistic. He started arguing with the Agents, swinging his arms and yelling as they were taking his box away. The next step for them was likely to take him to the ground, but before the head Guard gave the order he turned around to see who was watching. There was only you left.

He yelled at you and pointed to the exit door " GO !!! "   Likely the only person ever to go thru a Russian Customs without inspection of passport or suitcase.

<u>*You lived that picture then. Live it now.*</u>

119: GOD AFFIRMS:

I got home from an amazing trip and unbelievable spiritual journey.

Unbelievable, that was the way I was feeling. Did all of that really happen or was I just imagining it. Maybe I was fantasying as I did go to the "Holy Land". Surely it couldn't be true. Did I really talk with GOD or was it all just in my head.

I was driving into the parking lot at work listening to the radio catching up on the news on my first day back at work and

GOD said: *"Turn your CD on. I want to affirm that everything that happened, happened and I want you to know, that I am GOD."*

Oh man, I needed to get to work as I had been away for 5 weeks. What could ever be on my CD player that would do that ?
Would I have to maneuver, finesse or get real creative to make it work ? What if there was nothing related at all on the CD, it would just prove I'm making it all up?

I pulled into the parking lot and sat there. I turned the radio off and placed my figure over the CD button…And waited...

What had we discussed that needed affirmation:
1) That GOD was GOD. There are no other gods.
2) That Jesus, GOD, our Saviour, is the Only way.

I had recalled that I have a 5 CD player and that one of them was a part of about a 24 set disc of the Bible the others music. It had been awhile so I had no idea which one or where it would be playing.
I pressed the CD button and it was the tapes voice of GOD speaking vs a narrative section which is most of the Bible CD. So we got the bible CD and we have the actor's voice who reads GODS parts:
" I, even I, am Jehovah: and besides me there is no savior."
Isaiah 43:11.

I read the whole chapter and it was an amazing confirmation.
Thank you Lord, what a journey.

120: <u>WHAT IF I AM WRONG ABOUT EVERYTHING...</u>

So many things I still do not understand, but that is OK.

Someone asked me once, what if I am totally wrong and there is no GOD, no after life, no eternity. What if I am not a spirit but just a man who will one day die and return to dust? What if it was all just coincidence and my wild imagination?

I replied: "That will be fine."

I could not imagine living my life without believing what I believe. A GOD who cares enough about me and my day to day life, helping, guiding and protecting me. HE has given me purpose and hope, with that, a life worth living to the fullest.

So with all the miracles, conversations and interactions I have had so far in this journey, what do I believe?

<u>I hold to 3 truths as I tried to get it down to the simpliest basics:</u>

1) **There is a GOD.**
2) **That GOD cares about me.**
3) **That Jesus the Christ, the Son of GOD, His life, His death and His resurrection provided the pathway, the door, the bridge for me to be reunited with my HEAVENLY FATHER.**

All in all, my focus needs to be on the one MAIN THING:

To Love the LORD my GOD
with all my heart, my soul and my mind...
and to LOVE my neighbor (others) as myself.

121: The GRANDEST of ALL FINALE !!!

I was talking to GOD one day and I said, "I love the first story of this book and how it starts but what should the last story be, the **Grandest of all Finale**, will it have thunder and lightning, will I walk on water, will the heavens open and the sky be filled with Angels singing the Hallelujah Chorus ? "

GOD said, **"I will let you know when the time is right".**

This morning, being Christmas morning 2016 we had our breakfast and I was sitting down with my coffee in my comfortable chair and ready to open our presents.

GOD showed up and said: **"I have my present for you, I have the final story, the Grandest of all Finale"**

What timing as always, not just Christmas morning but for the past few days I was seriously thinking on killing the whole book.   The new gift gave me the motivation and focus to write the rest of the stories and yes, **Finish** this book after 25 years. It will likely be 25 years to the day, as I started on May 1, 1992 and expect to publish May 1, 2017.

GOD created me to have a relationship with HIM.
I rebelled and sought my own way, lost my focus and purpose.
The gift was the Christmas Story
that leads me to the Easter Story
which is my redemption story
and gets me on the pathway back.
The pathway on my **SPIRITUAL JOURNEY,**
to walk it with ALMIGHTY GOD,
MY HEAVENLY FATHER.

122: SUMMARY...

Yes, I did tell GOD he was wrong, I told GOD it was HIS fault, I told GOD to get lost, but I wonder if maybe we all do, not so much in our words but in our actions.

So far this has been an amazing journey.

I have seen GOD part the clouds to show me the amazing view.
GOD saved me from my fear in the depths of a dark cave.
I have seen GOD heal my loved ones.
I learned to follow GOD as HE built the Cumberland Boys Club.
GOD has taken me on a great adventure to Russia.
GOD met with me in the Holy Land.

I have felt GOD's wrath and that HE is jealous for my time and mind.
I have learned **to FORGIVE** as I am forgiven.
I have learned **to LOVE**, as I am loved unconditionally.

I have only started on this exciting eternal journey and the next great adventure GOD is now preparing me for.

Most of life is not spent on either the mountain top or deepest caves but on the day to day journey just putting one foot in front of the other at work, at play or at rest. The biggest gift of GOD is I can do this all with HIM and no matter the situation HE gives me the JOY, the PEACE, the LOVE and the ASSURANCE that I am not alone and that HE does have and is in control of OUR JOURNEY.

I woke up this morning and said:

"What do you have for us to do TODAY LORD ? !!!

Next Book.

Questions I have asked on my Spiritual Journey.

1) Who is right, Science or Creation, how old is the earth ?

2) What really happened, Creation or Evolution ?

3) Why would GOD kill the babies in Jericho and the flood ?

4) Reincarnation , predestination and other big words ?

5) What happens to those who never heard the gospel ?

6) What did GOD do before creation ?

7) Is the Bible really the Truth, then why so many beliefs ?

8) What about the Book of Enoch and other manuscripts ?

I originally had this part of this book but I can see it will take me at least another year to finish my stories on these questions. I must say, most of the answers, I never did learn in Sunday School and are not the same answer as I have read from any other Christian based writer.

I will look at answering the best I can from the Bible. The reason I think it is needed as I know so many that have walked away from their faith, as these questions have bothered them. I believe the Enemy uses the confusion of these questions to divide us where I believe the answer should unite us.

If you are interested, let me know.
Email: therockkelowna@gmail.com
I hope to have published by April 2018.

Made in the USA
Columbia, SC
01 May 2017